DIY Patterns by Pictures

Advanced Guide to Knitting Techniques, Stitches, and Patterns with Easy-to-Follow Steps and Illustrations

By

Maggie Samir

Copyrighted Material

Copyright © Autumn Leaf Publishing Press, 2019

Email: Publisher@AutumnLeafPub@gmail.com

All Rights Reserved.

Without limiting the rights under the copyright laws, no part of this publication may be reproduced, stored in or introduced into a retrieval system, or transmitted, in any form or by any means (electronic, mechanical, photocopying, recording or otherwise), without the prior written consent of the publisher of this book.

Autumn Leaf Publishing Press publishes its books and guides in a variety of electronic and print formats, Some content that appears in print may not be available in electronic format, and vice versa.

AUTUMN LEAF
PUBLISHING PRESS

Design & Illustration by Rebecca Johnson

First Edition

Contents

INTRODUCTION 1

READING A KNITTING PATTERN 3

KNIT A HEART CABLE USING A CHART 7

CHANGING COLORS IN KNITTING 22

    CHANGE COLOR HORIZONTALLY 22

        Flag Stitch *22*

    CHANGE COLOR VERTICALLY 29

    CHANGE COLOR WITH SLANT STYLE 35

    CHANGE COLOR DIAGONALLY 40

HOW TO WRITE OR DRAW IN KNITTING 57

    MAKING LETTERS 57

    DRAWING SHAPES 83

        Elephant Pattern *83*

FREE BONUS PATTERNS 98

    WINTER FLOWER 1 99

    WINTER FLOWER 2 100

    REINDEER 101

    CHRISTMAS TREE 102

    REINDEER AND TREE 103

    HAND-DRAWN REINDEER 104

    FREEFORM 105

    TIGER DECORATIVE 106

    BUTTERFLY 107

    HEART 108

Mouse	109
Owl	110
Strawberry	111
Dog	112
Rabbit	113
Swan	114
Cat	115
Ancient Egyptian Beetle	116
Nefertiti Queen	117
Sphinx	118
Ancient Egyptian Eye	119
Egyptian Ankh	120

LACE STITCHES 121

Drop Stitch (The Horizontal River)	121
Horizontal River, Alternative Method	126
The Vertical River	130
Herringbone Lace Rib Stitch	132
Simple Lace	134
Spider Web Lace	142
Turkish Lace Stitch	152
Broken Lace Stitch	154
Shells Lace Stitch	158
Fishtail Lace Stitch	160
Butterfly Stitch	164
Leaves Stitch	180
Bucket Stitch	183
Lace Heart Stitch	189
Old Shale	195
Stockinette Chevron	196
Lace Stitch	198

FINISHING THE ENDS 202

KNITTING A HAT 206

Make the Cuff 207
Make the Crown 208
Hat Pattern Variants and Decorations 210
Change Colors *211*
Pinstripe Hat Variation *211*
Pom-Poms *212*

MARY JANE SHOES/BABY BOOTIES 221

Basic Shoe Pattern 222

DROP STITCH SCARF 236

Basic Scarf Pattern 236

GARTER STITCH BABY BLANKET 242

Basic Blanket Pattern 243

CONCLUSION 252

Introduction

I can remember sitting with my dear Grandma Mary on Sunday afternoons at her house surrounded by endless balls of yarn. My favorite item of clothing was a sweater she knitted for me one year. I wore it until it was full of holes!

My Grandmother was very patient with an overly eager 10 year old me. She took each step of showing me how to knit slowly. She carefully described each knit, purl, and yarn over in a way where I could keep up.

As I got older, I never lost that love of creating something meaningful with my own two hands. I loved making my own clothing, and gifts for others that you would never find in a big box store.

I can recall in my early twenties, when I was pregnant with my oldest daughter, how I was determined to make her a baby blanket. I would work on it day and night, thinking about swaddling her chubby little arms and legs into the plush, soft, blanket that her mommy made by hand for her.

My daughter is preparing to move out on her own and she still has that pink and white blanket!

In this book, I hope to share this love of knitting with the world.

I will show you more advanced knitting techniques, so if you're just now starting out, I would suggest that you put this book down now, and grab a copy of my first knitting tutorial book in this "Knitting by Pictures" series.

Thank you so much for reading this book. I hate to be "that author," but it would mean so much to me if you could leave a review about this book (or the series) wherever you purchased this book. I am hoping to turn this crafty little hobby into something more and your review will help me tremendously.

Happy Knitting!

Reading a Knitting Pattern

Here's the key to reading a cable knitting pattern:

BO= bind off.

Btwn=between.

CC= contrasting color.

CN= cable needle.

CO=cast on.

dpn(s) = double pointed needle(s).

K= knit

K1b= knit through the back loop.

K2tog= knit 2 together.

K3tog= knit 3 together.

KFB= knit in front and back of the stitch.

Lp(s) = loop(s).

M1= make one.

M2= make two.

MC= main color.

P= purl.

P1b= purl through the back loop.

P2sso= pass 2 slipped stitch over.

PU= pick up.

Rep= repeat.

RH= right hand.

Rnd= round.

RS= right side.

SK2P= slip 1, K2tog, pass SL St over.

SKP= slip1, knit 1, pass slipped stitch over.

SL= slip.

SL St= slip stitch.

Slip1- Knit1 – passo= slip1, knit 1, pass slip stitch over.

SSK= slip, slip, knit, knit the two slipped stitches together.

St st = stockinette.

tbl=   through the back loop.

tog= together.

Ws= wrong side.

wyib=with yarn in back.

wyif= with yarn in front.

YO= yarn over.

C4B= SL 2 stitches hold them to the back, K2, K2 from CN (cable needle).

C4F= SL 2 stitches hold them to the front, K2, K2 from CN (cable needle).

CR4B= SL 2 stitches hold them to the back, K2, P2 from CN (cable needle).

CL4F=SL 2 stitches hold them to the front, P2, K2 from CN (cable needle).

CR3B=SL 1 stitch hold it to the back, K2, P1 from CN (cable needle).

CL3F= SL 2 stitches hold them to the front, P1, K2 from CN (cable needle).

Knit a Heart Cable Using a Chart

	Knit on both RS and WS
	Knit on RS and purl on WS
ℓ	Purl on RS and knit on WS
	C4B: slip 2 hold back, K2 and K2 from cable needle
	C4F: slip 2 hold front, K2 and K2 from cable needle
	CR4B: slip 2 hold back, K2 and P2 from cable needle
	CR4F: slip 2 hold front, P2 and K2 from cable needle
	CR3B: : slip 1 hold back, K2 and P1 from cable needle
	CR3F: slip 2 hold front, P1 and K2 from cable needle

Cast 24 stitches for this panel. The cable consists of 12 stitches and 4 stitches on each side of it with 2 stitches for each edge.

Row 1: The right side (K2, P4, K2, C4B, C4F, K2, P4, K2) repeat until the end of the row.

The first row (the right side): (K2, P4, K2, C4B
C4B= SL 2 stitches hold them to the back, K2, K2 from CN (cable needle).

C4F

C4F = SL 2 stitches hold them to the front, K2, K2 from CN (cable needle).

The first row (the right side):
(K2, P4, K2, C4B, C4F, K2, P4, K2)

C4F hold it to the front
C4B hold it to the back
K2 P4 K2 P4 K2

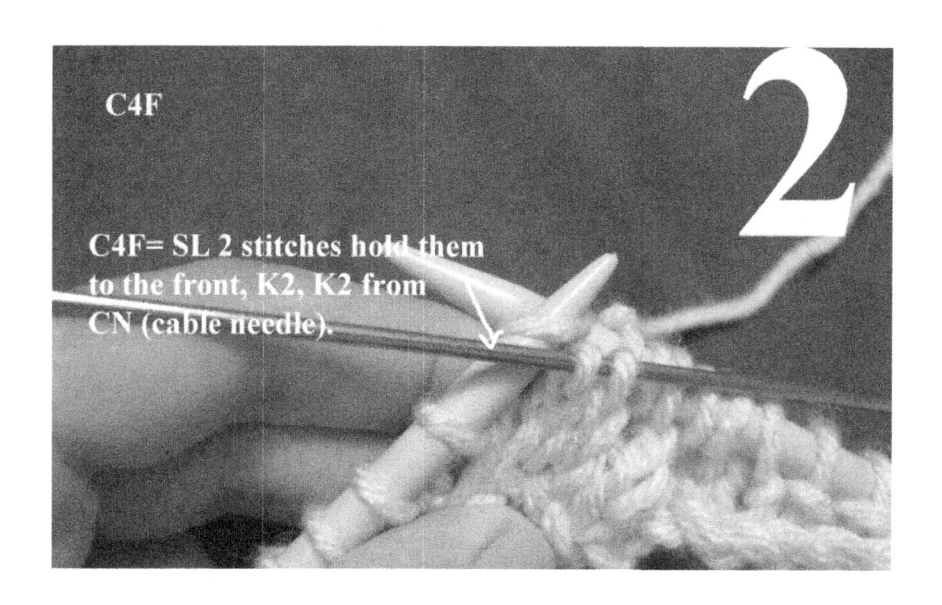

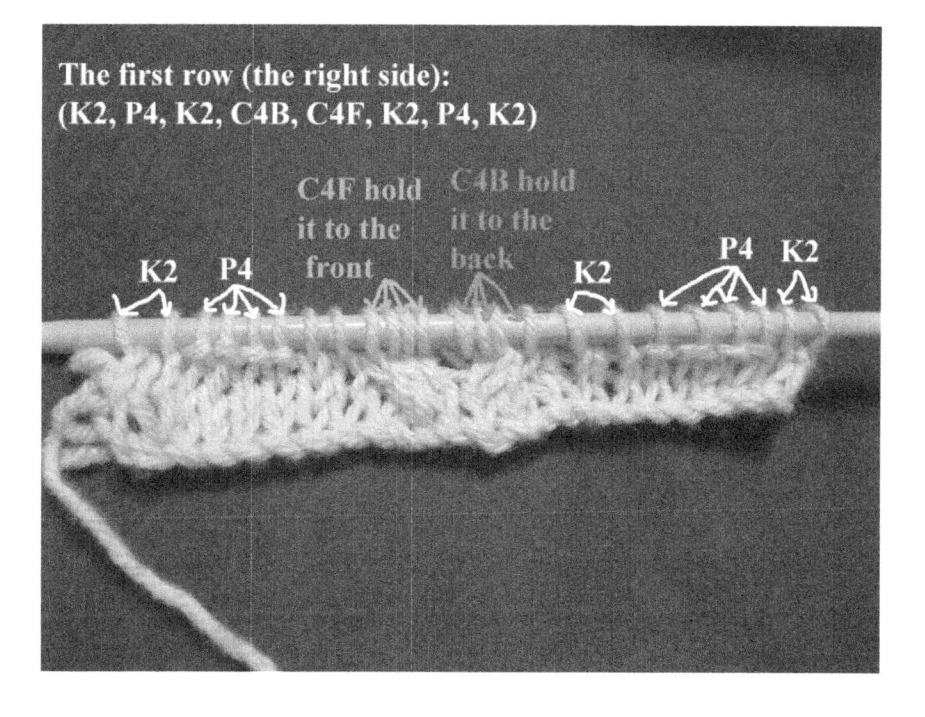

Row 2: The wrong side (K6, P12, K6)

> The second row (the wrong side): (K6, P12, K6)

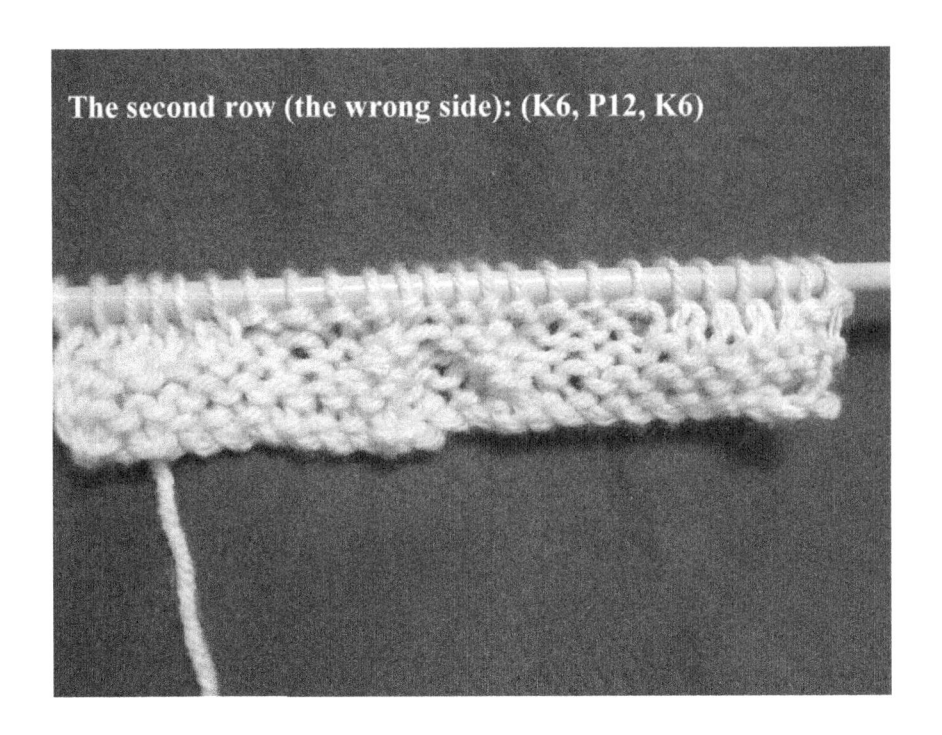

Cable heart repeat rows: **Row 3:** K2, P4, CR4B, K4, CL4F, P4, K2.

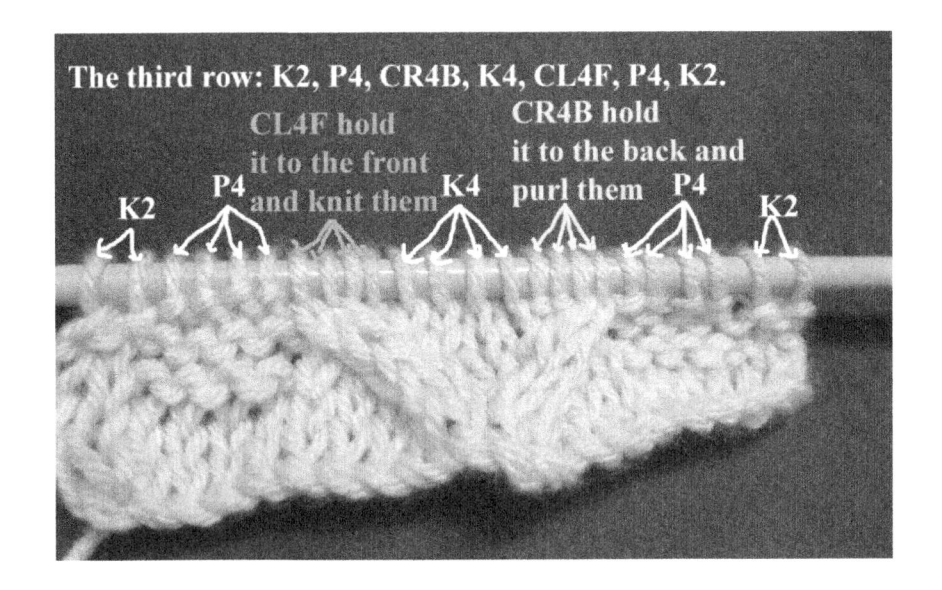

> The third row: K2, P4, CR4B, K4, CL4F, P4, K2.
> CL4F hold it to the front and knit them
> CR4B hold it to the back and purl them
> K2   P4   K4   P4   K2

The third row: K2, P4, CR4B

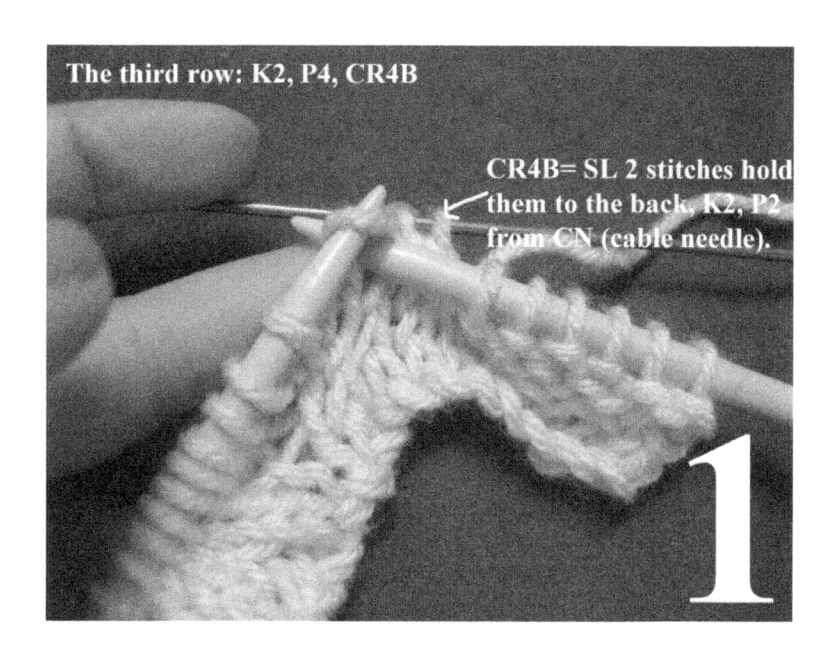

CR4B= SL 2 stitches hold them to the back, K2, P2 from CN (cable needle).

CL4F

CL3F= SL 2 stitches hold them to the front, P1, K2 from CN (cable needle).

Row 4 K6, P2, K2, P4, K2, P2, K6.

The fourth row: K6, P2, K2, P4, K2, P2, K6

Row 5: K2, P3, CR3B, P2, C4B, P2, CL3F, P3, K2.

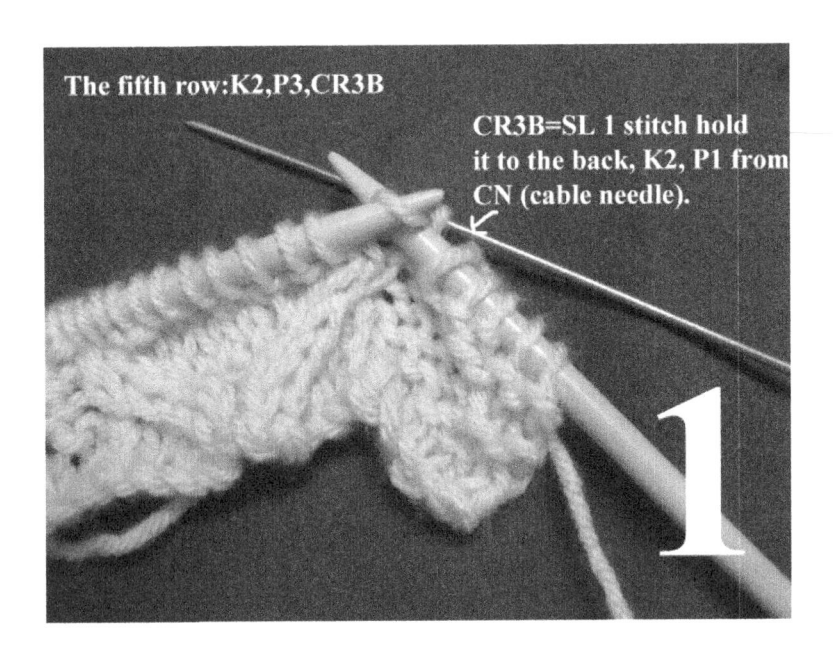

The fifth row: K2, P3, CR3B

CR3B=SL 1 stitch hold it to the back, K2, P1 from CN (cable needle).

C4B

C4B= SL 2 stitches hold them to the back, K2, K2 from CN (cable needle).

CL3F

CL3F= SL 2 stitches hold them to the front, P1, K2 from CN (cable needle).

The fifth row: K2,P3,CR3B,P2,C4B,P2,CL3F,P3,K2.

Row 6: K5, P2, K3, P4, K3, P2, K5.

The sixth row: K5, P2, K3, P4, K3, P2, K5.

Row 7: K2, P2, CR3B, P3, K4, P3, CL3F, P2, K2.

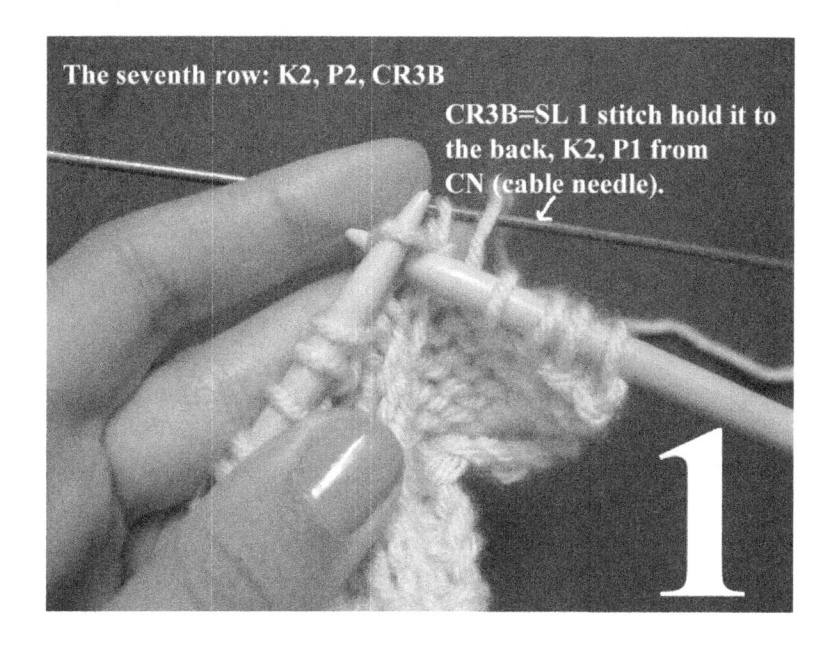

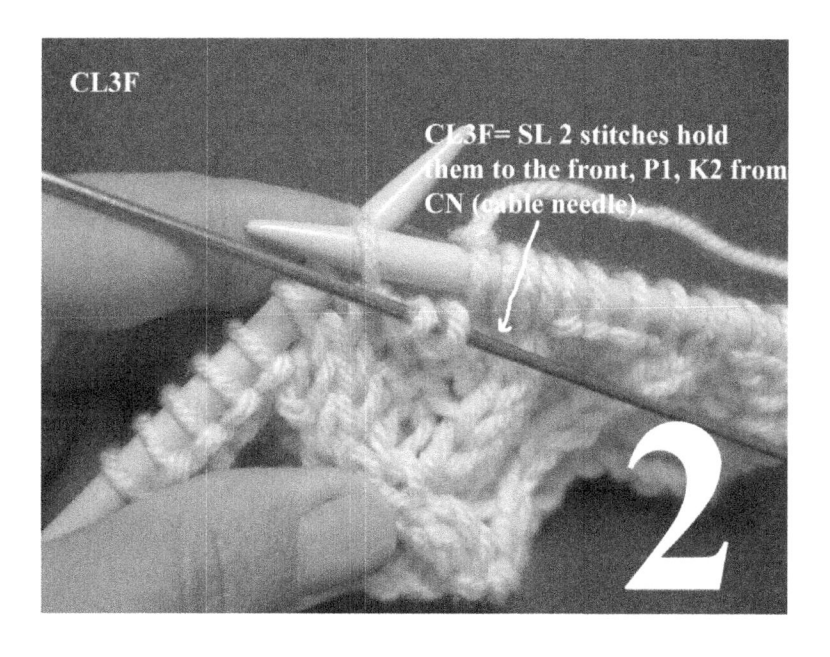

The seventh row: K2, P2, CR3B

CR3B=SL 1 stitch hold it to the back, K2, P1 from CN (cable needle).

CL3F

CL3F= SL 2 stitches hold them to the front, P1, K2 from CN (cable needle).

The seventh row: K2, P2, CR3B, P3, K4, P3, CL3F, P2, K2

Row 8: K4, P2, K4, P4, K4, P2, K4.

The eighth row: K4, P2, K4, P4, K4, P2, K4.

Row 9: K2, P2, K2, P4, C4B, P4, K2, P2, K2.

The ninth row: K2, P2, K2, P4, C4B

C4B= SL 2 stitches hold them to the back, K2, K2 from CN (cable needle).

The ninth row: K2, P2, K2, P4, C4B, P4, K2, P2, K2.

Row 10: K4, P2, K4, P4, K4, P2, K4.

Row 11: K2, P2, CL4F, C4B, C4F, CR4B, P2, K2.

C4B

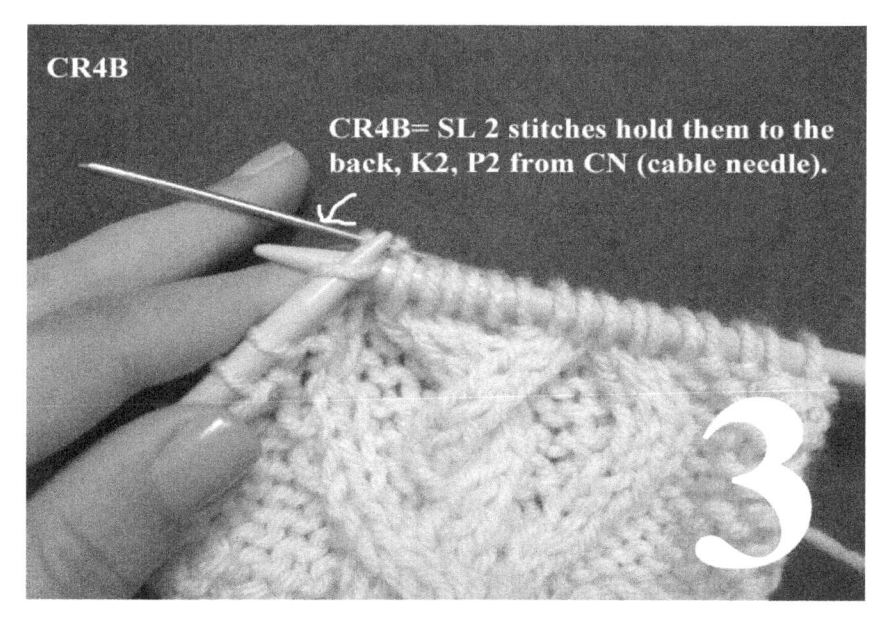

C4B = SL 2 stitches hold them to the back, K2, K2 from CN (cable needle).

CR4B

CR4B = SL 2 stitches hold them to the back, K2, P2 from CN (cable needle).

The eleventh row: K2, P2, CL4F, C4B, C4F, CR4B, P2, K2.

Row 12: K6, P12, K6.

The twelfth row: K6, P12, K6.

Continue this pattern repeating the cable heart rows from row three to row twelve.

Changing Colors in Knitting

In this chapter, we will learn how to join a new color, and this will be amazing!

Learning this skill, you will be able to create your own unique pattern. So let's start!

Change Color Horizontally

First I will show you how to join a new color at the beginning of the row.

Flag Stitch

One way to change color at the start of a row is to use the flag stitch.

The flag stitch combines just the knit and purl stitches to produce a beautiful layered, textured effect.

The flag stitch is excellent for adding some relief, and texture to large projects, such as cardigans or blankets.

23

You have to cast on a number of stitches that can be divided by 6.

Row 1: Use color A (K5, P) repeat to the end of the row.

Row 2: Use color A (K2, P4) repeat to the end of the row.

Row 3: Use color A (K3, P3) repeat to the end of the row.

Row 4: Use color A (K4, P2) repeat to the end of the row.

Row 5: Use color A (K1, P5) repeat to the end of the row.

Row 6: Use color A. Knit all the stitches. Cut the yarn and weave the ends.

Continue in this manner, repeating the six rows from the first row. Switch to color B by joining color B.

Make a slip knot with color B and knit with it then cut the A yarn.

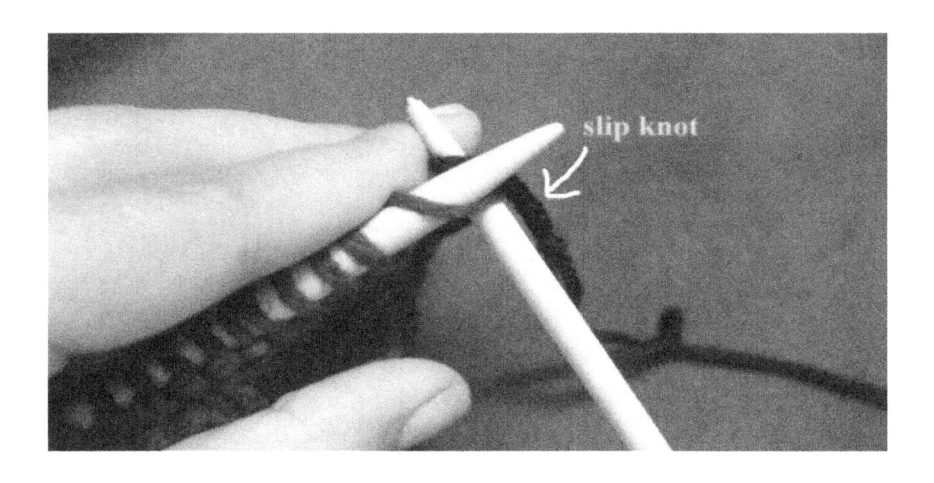

Weave the ends. Hold color A between your middle and index finger.

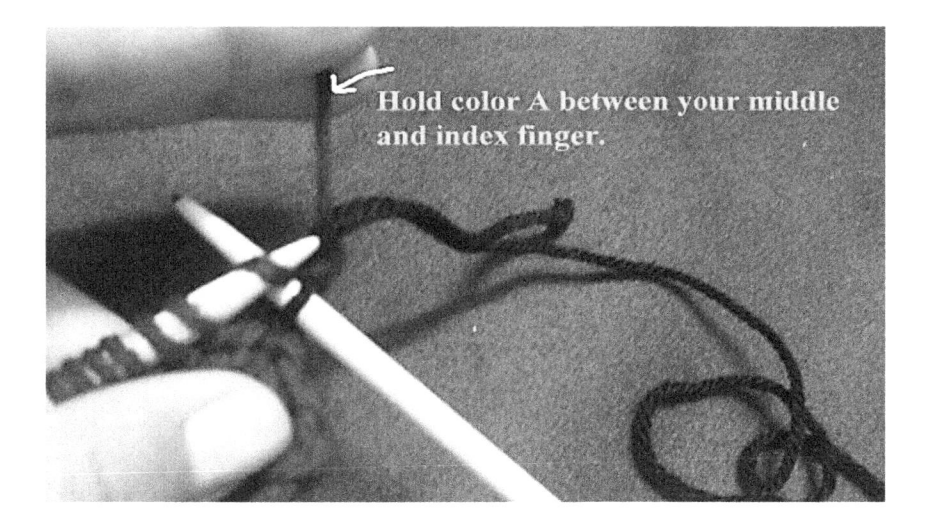

Knit the next stitch with color B using the tail and the working yarn to secure it.

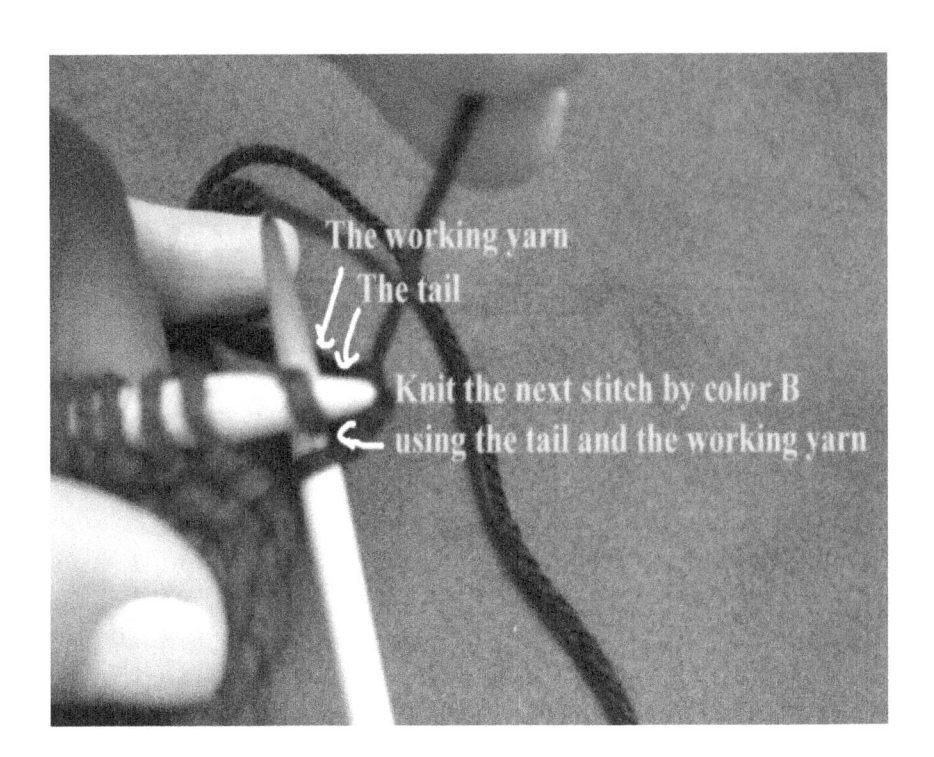

Hold the A yarn up.

Knit it under the back of the A yarn.

Wrap to the front of color A.

Knit the third stitch by the same way until you hide the tail of color A.

Hold the A yarn up and knit under the back of the A yarn

1

then warp to the front of color A

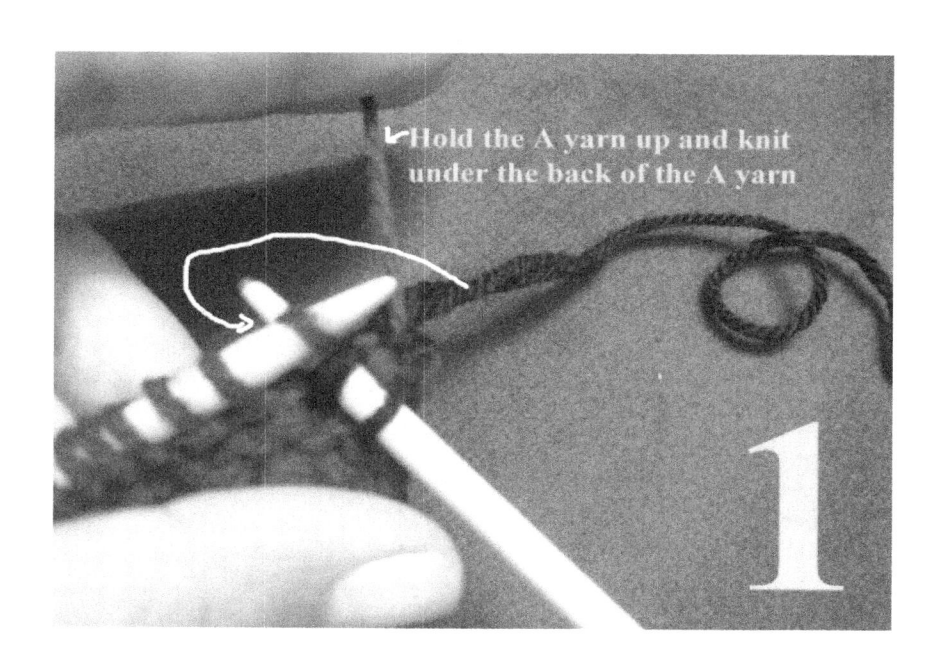

2

27

Done hiding the tail

3

The wrong side

After another six rows, alternate with color A.

Change Color Vertically

I will demonstrate this method using the stockinette stitch. You will be able to join many colors together.

29

Changing colors vertically requires twisting the two different yarns around each other to avoid creating a hole.

To begin, cast on the desired number of stitches.

Row 1: The right side.

Knit some stitches with color A unit you reach the stitch that you want to be connected with color B.

Hold color A between your middle and index finger.

Make a slip knot with color B and knit the next stitch through it.

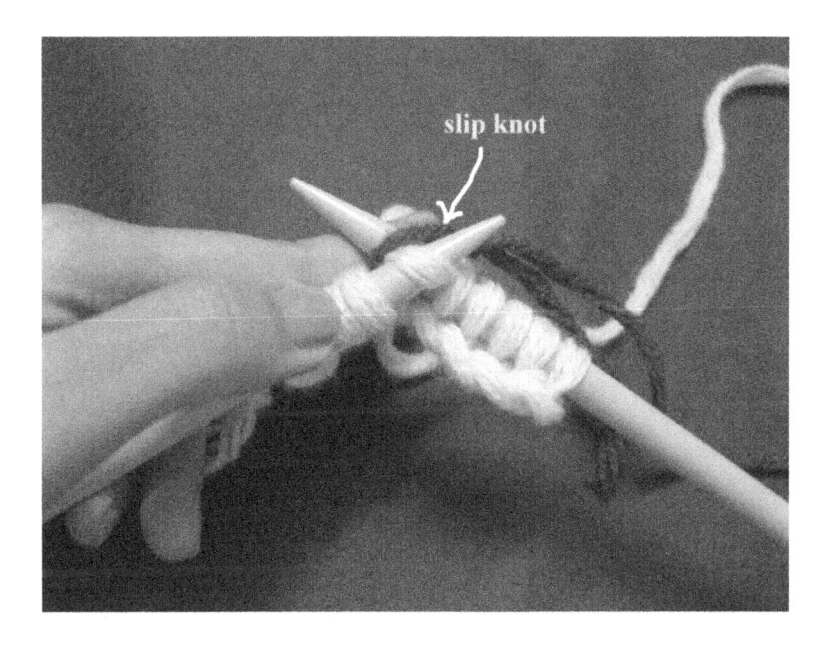

Knit the next stitch by twisting color A over and to the left of color B. Bring color B up and to the right of color A. Knit the stitch with color B.

Leave the color A strand alone. Continue knitting with color B until the end of the row.

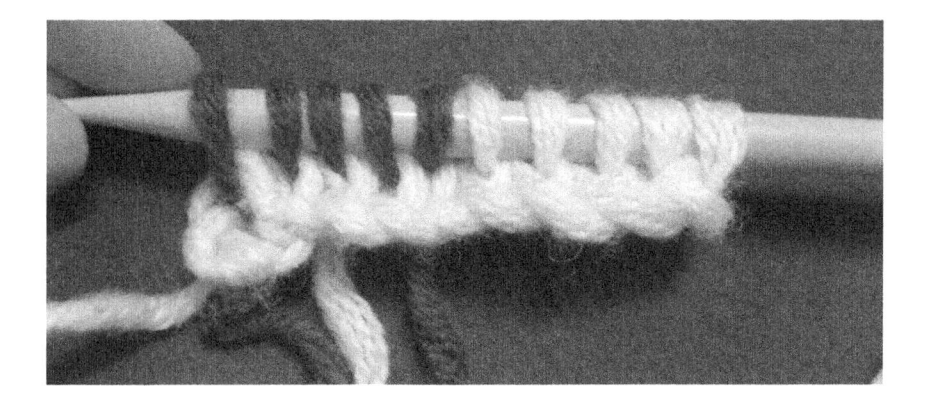

Row 2: Purl with color B to the point of color change. Twist color B over, and to the left of color A. Bring color A up and to the right of color B. Purl the stitch with color A.

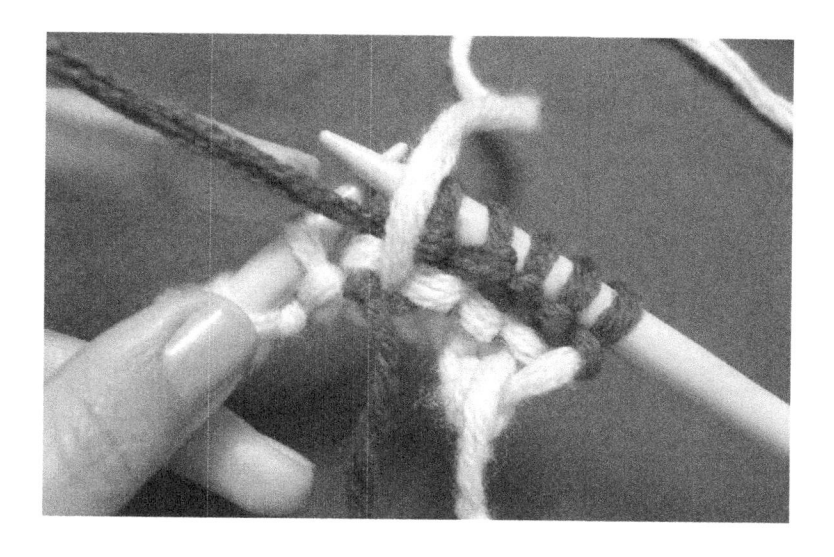

33

Continue purling with color A until the end of the row.

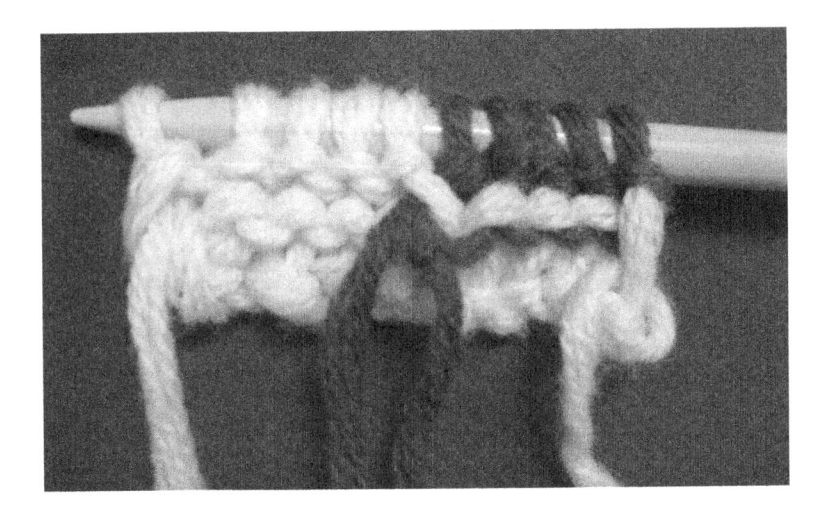

Do the same with all the next rows.

The wrong side

Change Color with Slant Style

Cast on the desired number of stitches.

Row 1: Knit some stitches with color A until you reach the stitch you want to be knitted with color B.

Hold color A between your middle and index finger. Make a slip knot with color B.

Knit the next stitch through it.

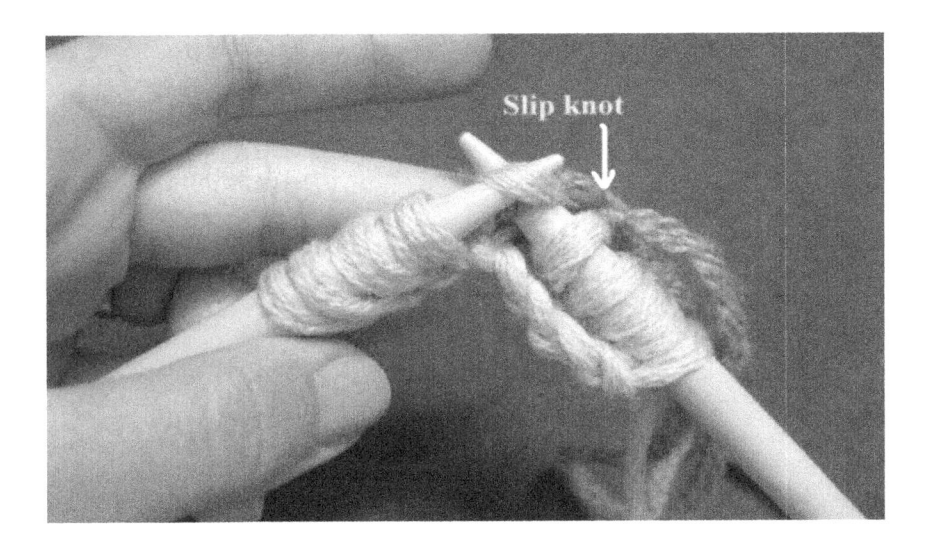

Knit the next stitch by twisting color A over and to the left of color B.

Bring color B up and to the right of color A.

Knit the stitch with color B.

> Bring color B up and to the right of color A and knit the stitch with color B.

Leave the color A strand. Continue knitting with color B until the end of the row.

Row 2: With color B, purl the number of stitches equal to the number of stitches that you knitted in the previous row.

Add one stitch that will be the base of the slant.

Twist color B over and to the left of color A.

Bring color A up and to the right of color B.

Purl the stitch with color A.

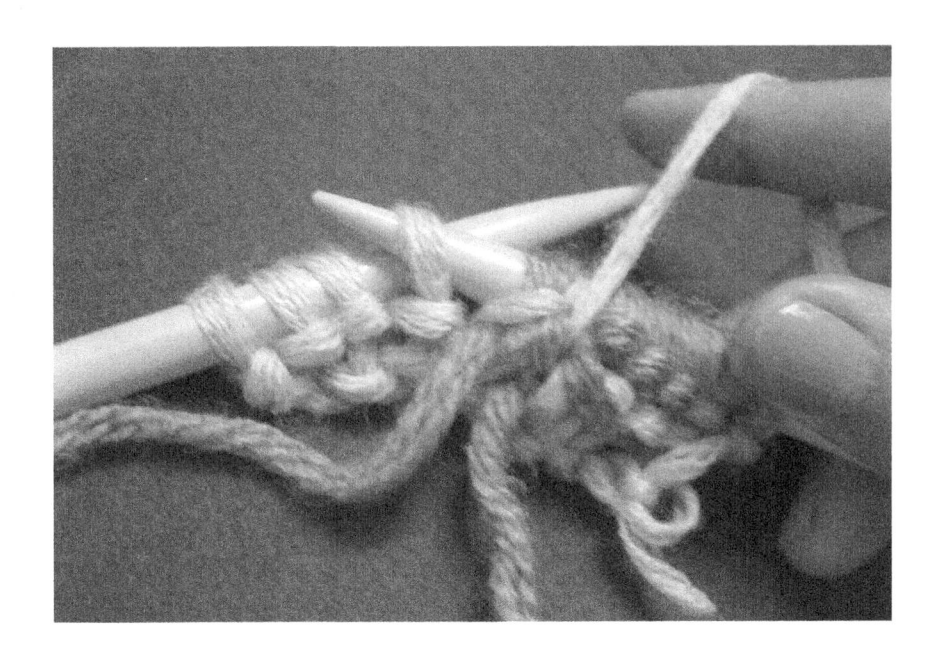

Continue purling with color A until the end of the row.

Row 3: With color A, knit the number of stitches equal to the number of stitches that you knitted in the first row. Subtract one stitch. Continue making the required slant.

Don't forget to twist color B over and to the left of color A at the back of the work. Bring color A up and to the right of color B. Knit the stitch with color A.

Row 4: Do the same as **Row 2**.

Row 5: Do the same as **Row 3**.

Repeat the even rows as you did the second row and the odd rows as the third row until the end of your pattern.

Change Color Diagonally

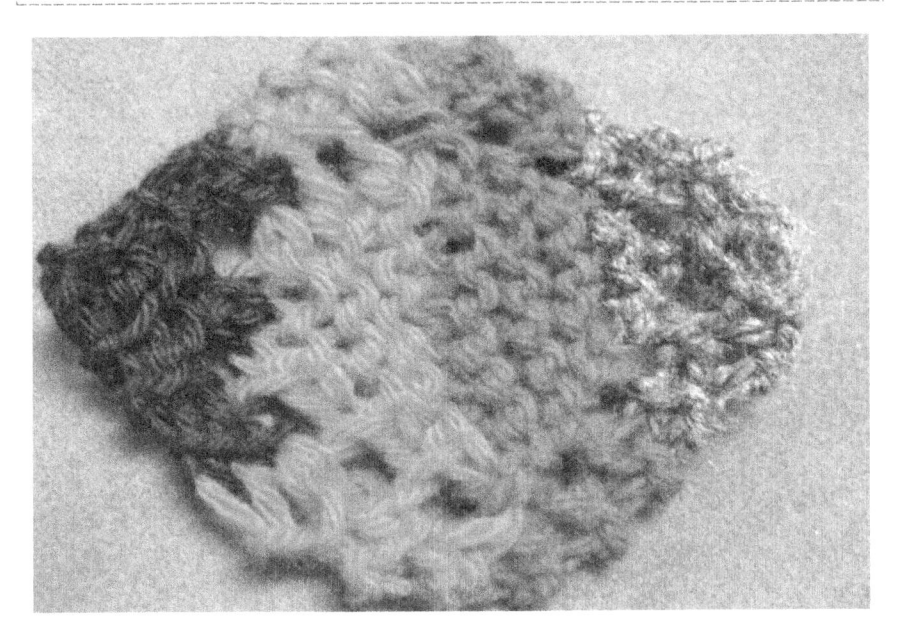

40

Cast on 3 stitches with color A.

Row 1: Knit all stitches with color A.

Row 2: Increase with color A.

Use the KFB (knit front and back) method. K1, KFB.

Now you have 5 stitches.

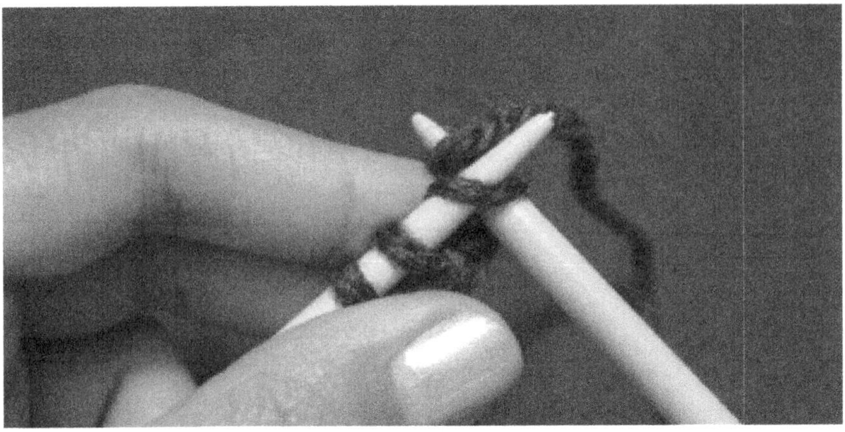

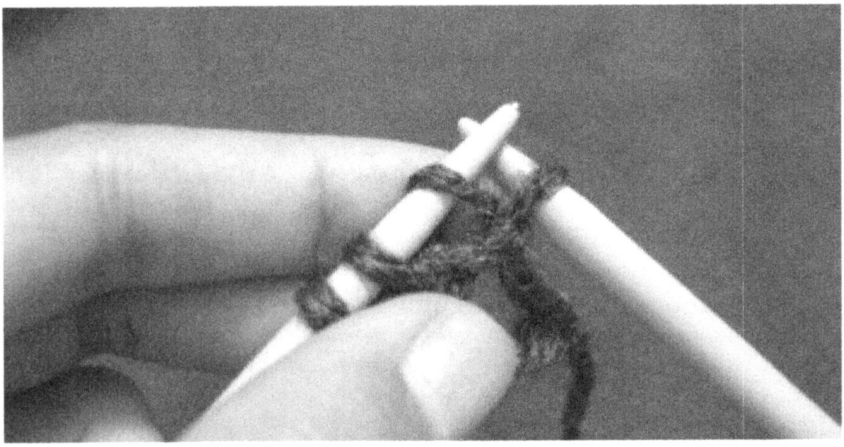

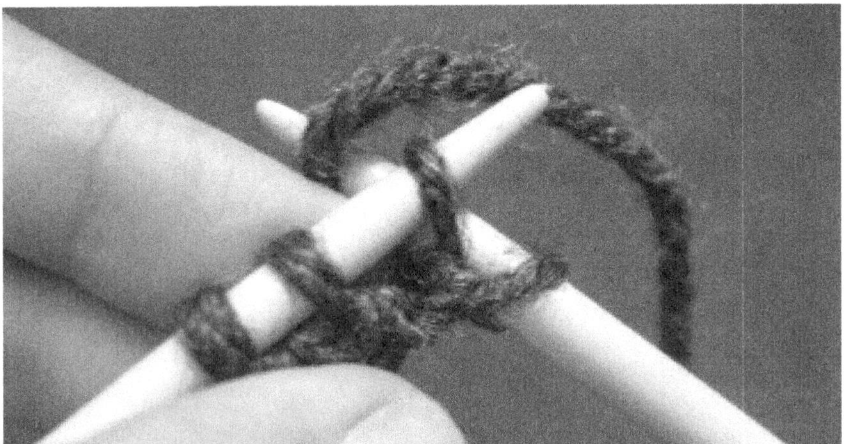

Row 3: Knit all stitches with color A.

Row 4: K2, YO, K1, YO, K2. Now you have 7 stitches.

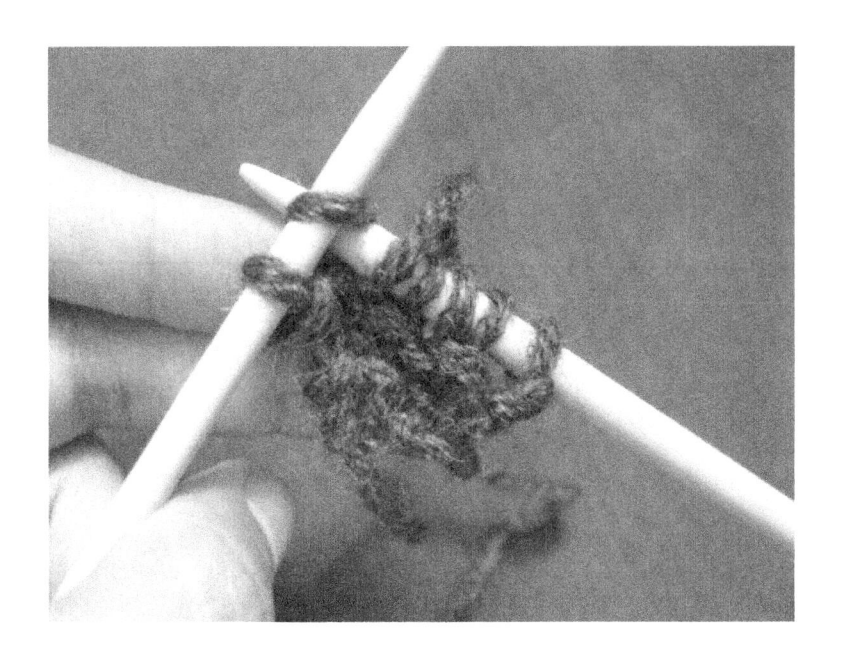

Row 5: Knit all stitches with color A.

Row 6: K2, YO. Knit until you reach the last 2 stitches. YO, K2. Now you have 9 stitches

Cut the yarn. Hide it by knitting it in the back.

Join color B.

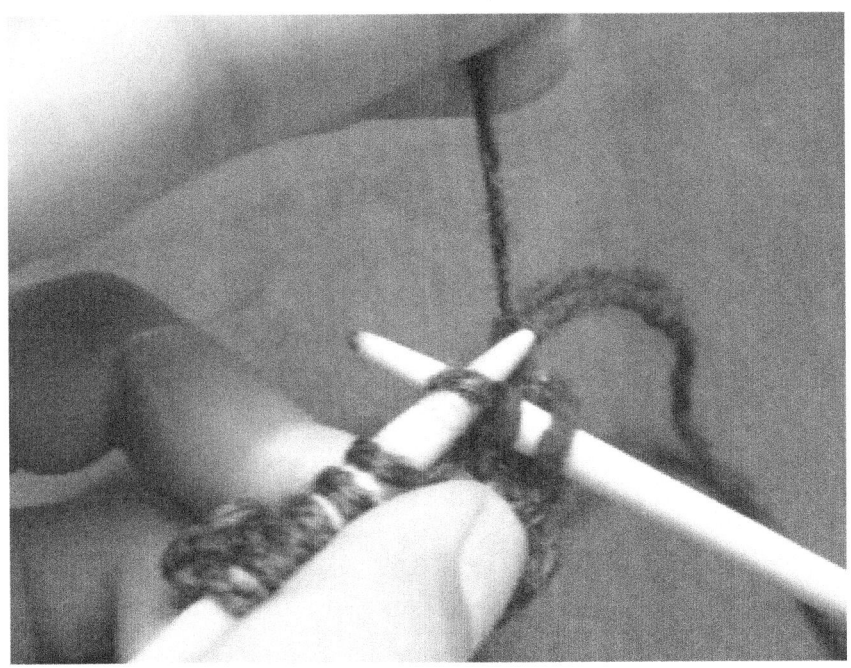

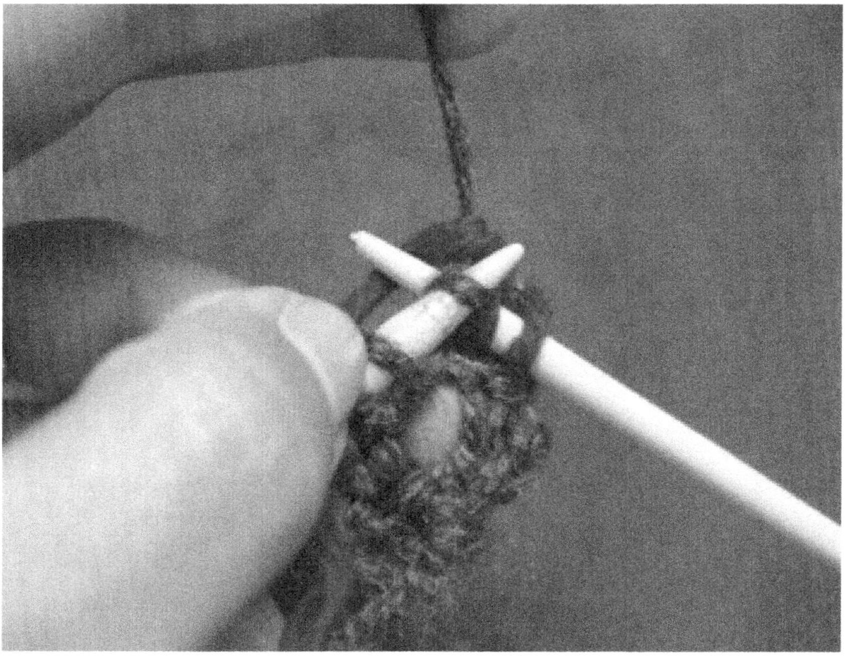

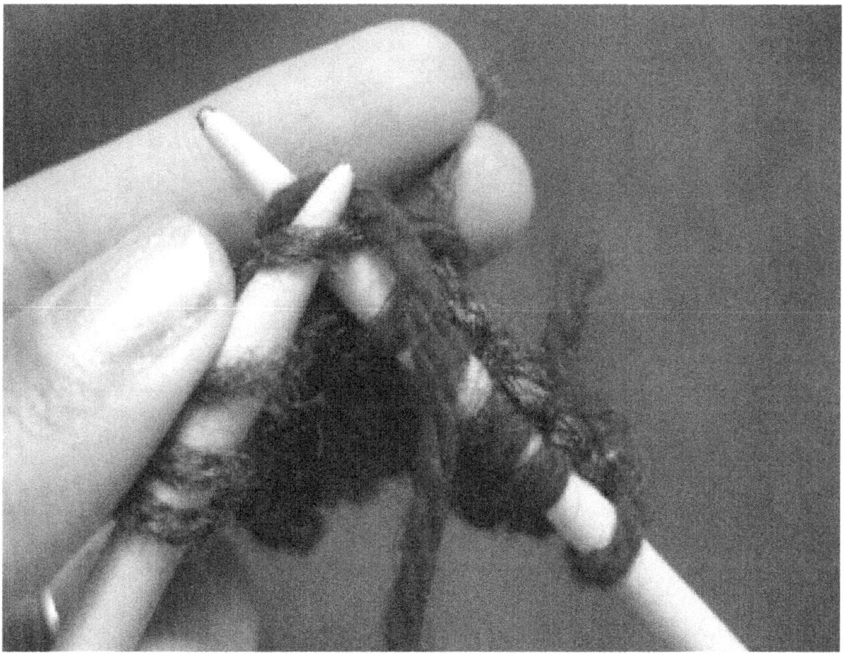

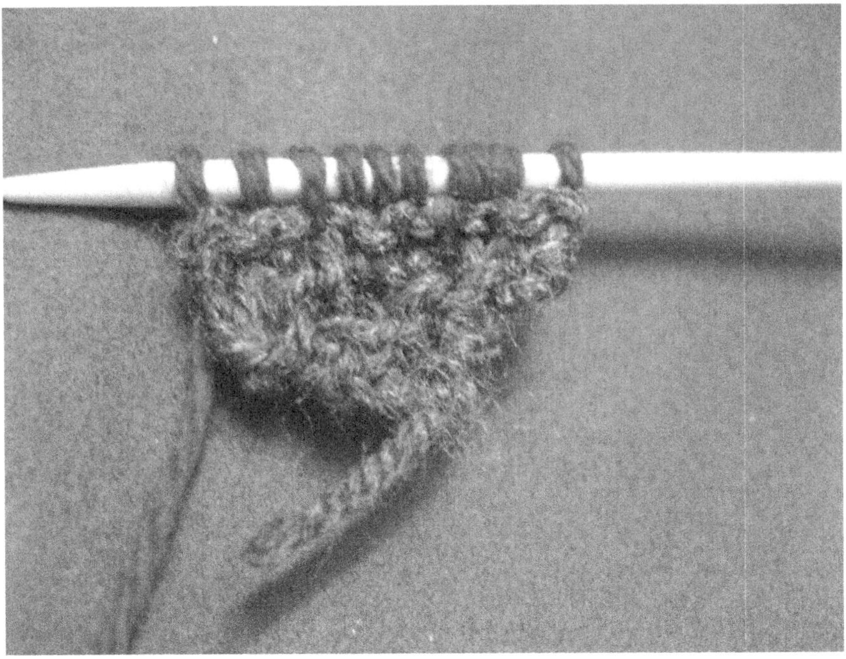

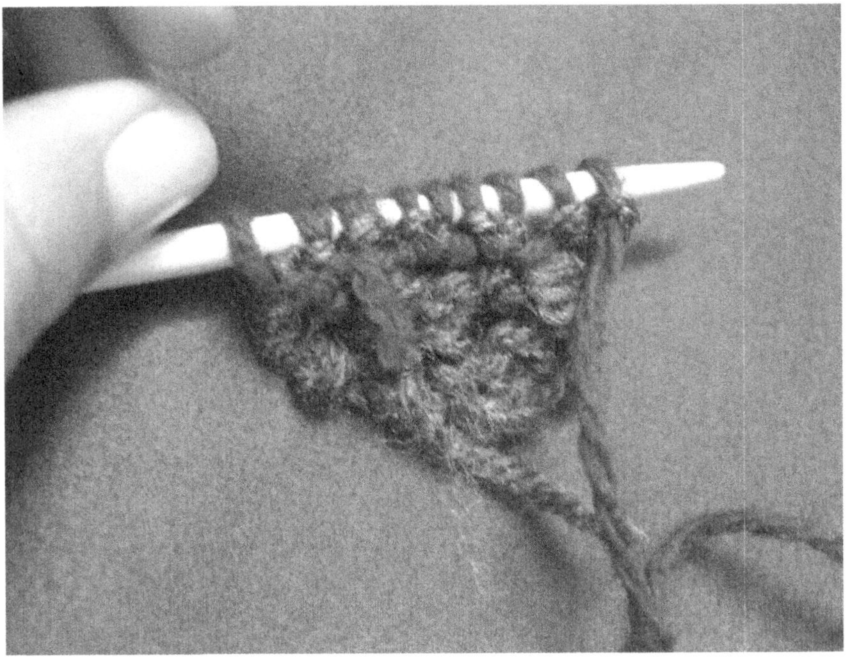

Repeat **Row 5 and 6** three times to **Row 12** with color B.

You can increase until you reach the desired pattern. For this example, cut the yarn and hide it. Join color C and start decreasing.

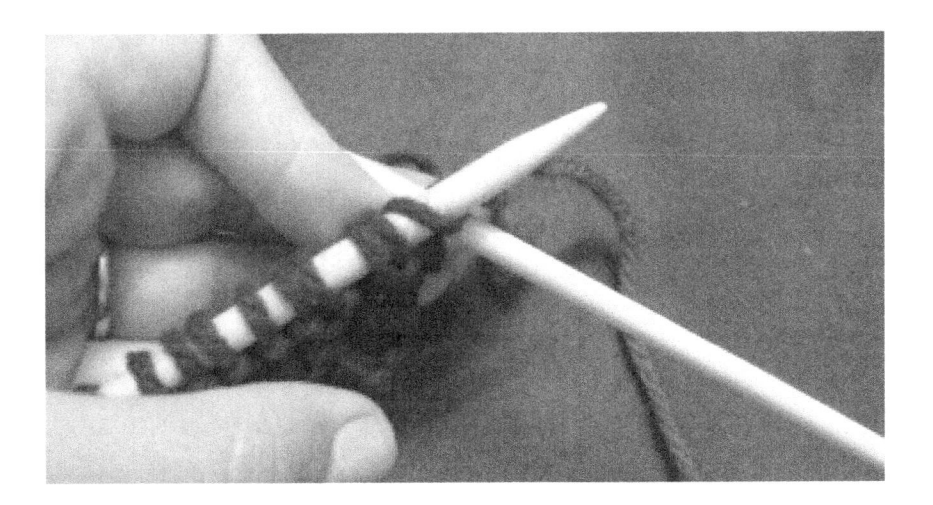

50

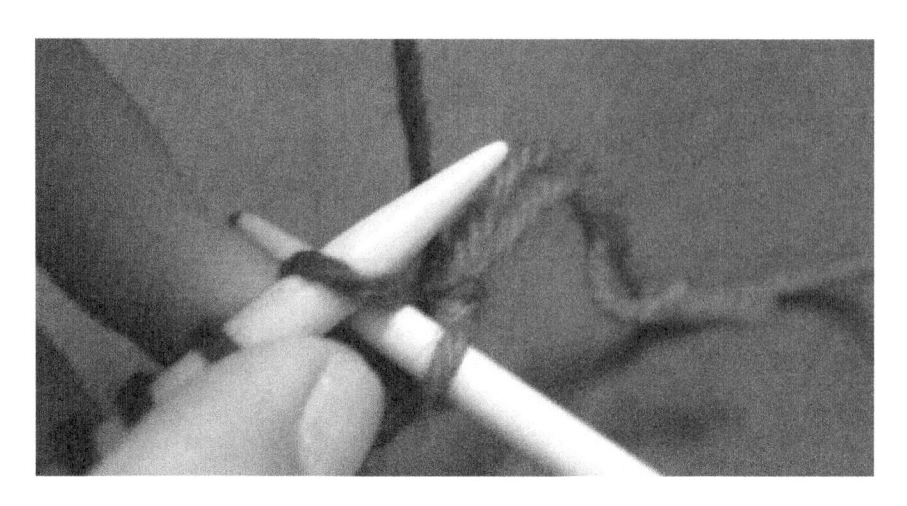

Row 13: Knit all stitches with color C.

Row 14: Using color C (K1, SSK, YO, K2tog, knit to the last five stitches, SSK, YO, K2tog, K1).

Row 15: Knit all stitches with color C.

Row 16: With color C (K1, SSK, YO, K2tog, knit to the last five stitches, SSK, YO, K2tog, K1).

Row 17: Knit all stitches with color C.

Row 18: With color C (K1, SSK, YO, K2tog, knit to the last five stitches, SSK, YO, K2tog, K1).

Notice a decrease with six rows and increase six rows. If you increase more, you have to decrease rows equal to the increased rows.

Cut the yarn and hide it. Join color D.

Row 19: Knit all stitches with color D.

Row 20: With color D [K1, SSK, YO, SK2P (slip1, K2tog, pass slip stitch over),YO, K2tog, K1).

Row 21: Knit all stitches with color D.

Row 22: With color D (K1, SSK, K1, K2tog, K1).

Row 23: Knit all stitches with color D.

Row 24: With color D (K1, SK2P, and K1). Bind off. Cut the yarn.

Weave the end by using a crochet hook to hide it.

hide the tail of the end

hide the tail of the beginning.

The wrong side

The right side

How to Write or Draw in Knitting

In this chapter, you will be able to write your name or a beautiful quote on your knitting or create cute drawings called jacquard.

Making Letters

Here's the pattern I will use to write Maggie on my project.

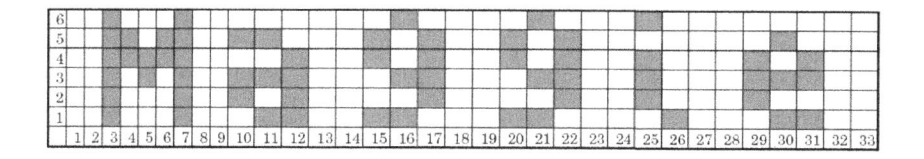

Apply this method to a project that uses the stockinette stitch.

Choose color A for your work and color B for the letters. Read the chart starting from the bottom right-hand corner.

Note that in flat knitting, read the chart from the left side in even rows and from the right in the odd rows.

Conversely, in round knitting, read every row from right to left.

Knit 6 rows as a border. Start from the seventh row to apply the pattern.

Read the chart from the bottom right-hand corner.

<u>Row 1:</u>

- ❖ K2 with color A

- ❖ K2 by joining color B

- ❖ K3 with color A

- ❖ K1 with color B

- K4 with color A

- K2 with color B

- K3 with color A

- K2 with color B

- K2 with color A

- K2 with color B

- K3 with color A

- K1 with color B

- K3 with color A

- K1 with color B

- K2 with color A

Make a slip knot

Cross A over B

Row 2:

- ❖ P2 with color A

- ❖ P1 with color B

- ❖ P3 with color A

- ❖ P1 with color B

- ❖ P2 with color A

- ❖ P1 with color B

- P1 with color A

- P1 with color B

- P4 with color A

- P1 with color B

- P4 with color A

- P1 with color B

- P2 with color A

- P1 with color B

- P3 with color A

- P1 with color B

- P4 with color A

Bring Yarn A

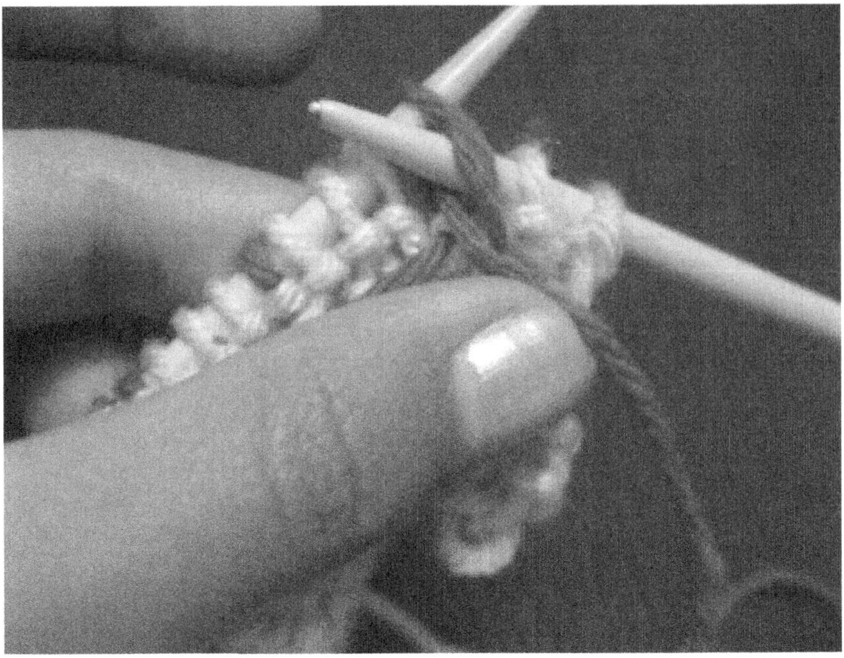

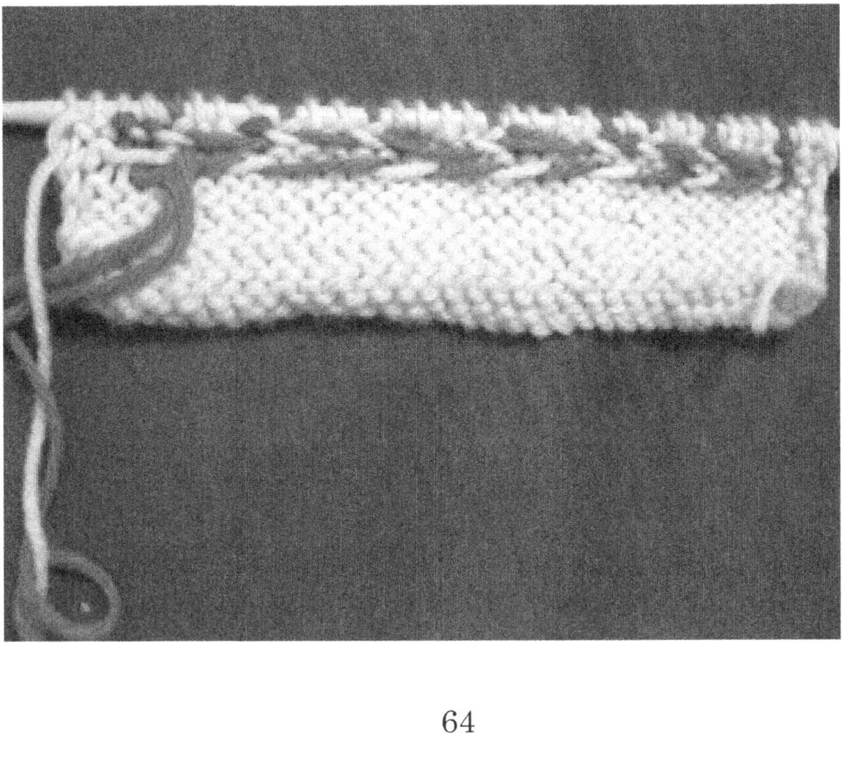

Row 3:

- ❖ K2 with color A

- ❖ K3 with color B

- ❖ K3 with color A

- ❖ K1 with color B

- ❖ K2 with color A

- ❖ K2 with color B

- ❖ K3 with color A

- ❖ K2 with color B

- ❖ K3 with color A

- ❖ K3 with color B

- ❖ K2 with color A

- ❖ K1 with color B

- ❖ K1 with color A

- ❖ K1 with color B

- ❖ K1 with color A

- ❖ K1 with color B

- ❖ K2 with color A.

Bring Yarn A to the left

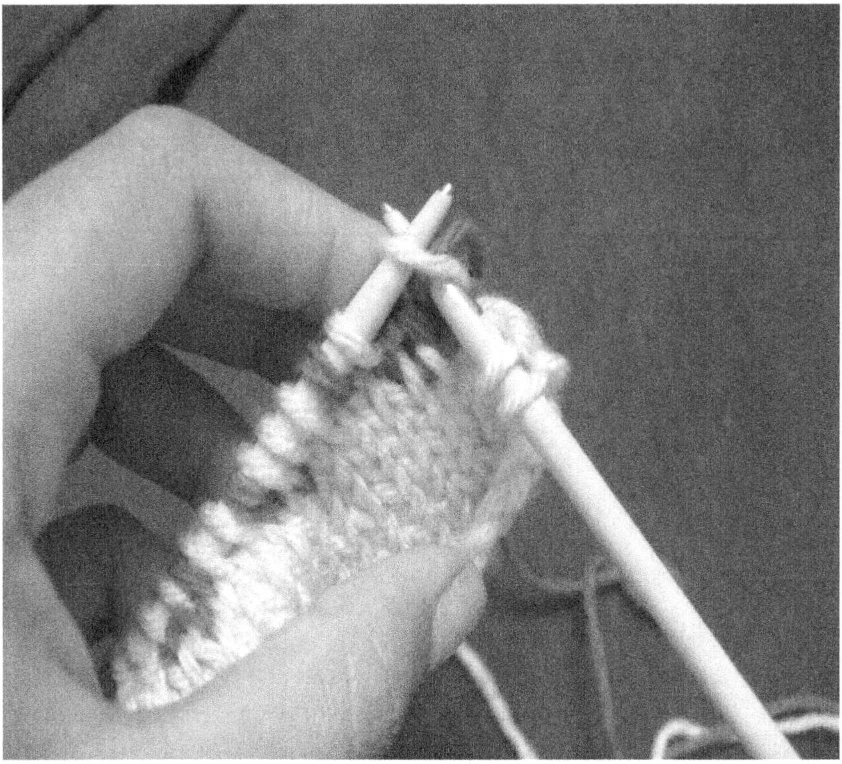

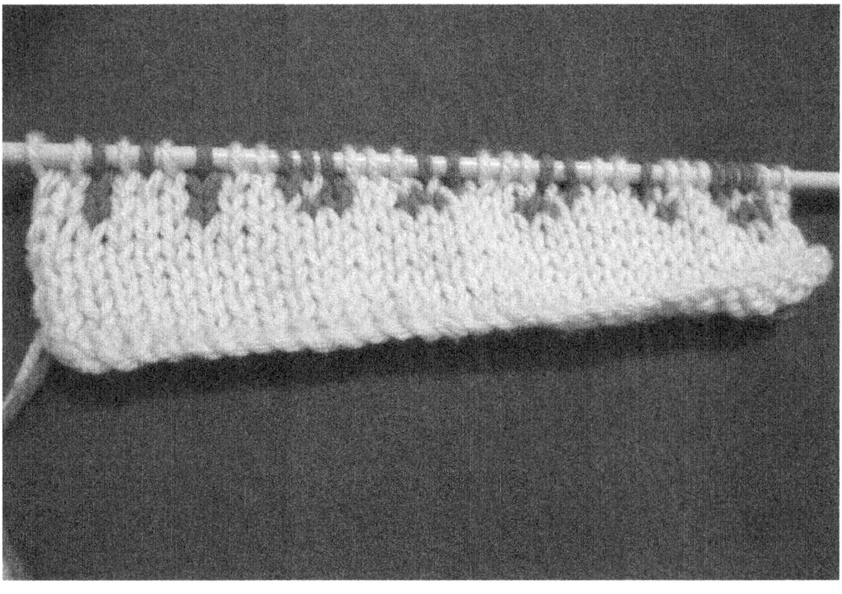

Row 4:

- P2 with color A

- P5 with color B

- P4 with color A

- P1 with color B

- P2 with color A

- P1 with color B

- P1 with color A

- P1 with color B

- P2 with color A

- P1 with color B

- P1 with color A

- ❖ P1 with color B

- ❖ P3 with color A

- ❖ P1 with color B

- ❖ P1 with color A

- ❖ P1 with color B

- ❖ P2 with color A

- ❖ P1 with color B

- ❖ P3 with color A

- ❖ P1 with color B

- ❖ P1 with color A

- ❖ P1 with color B

- ❖ P2 with color A

Bring Yarn A to the left

Row 5:

- ❖ K3 with color A

- ❖ K1 with color B

- ❖ k7 with color A

- ❖ K1 with color B

- ❖ k1 with color A

- ❖ K1 with color B

- K2 with color A
- K1 with color B
- K1 with color A
- K1 with color B
- K3 with color A
- K2 with color B
- K2 with color A
- K2 with color B
- K1 with color A
- K2 with color B
- K2 with color A

Bring Yarn B to the left

Row 6:

- P2 with color A

- P1 with color B

- P3 with color A

- P1 with color B

- P8 with color A

- ❖ P1 with color B

- ❖ P4 with color A

- ❖ P1 with color B

- ❖ P3 with color A

- ❖ P1 with color B

- ❖ P8 with color A

Cut color B and tie the tail with the end yarn twice. Weave the ends with a crochet hook.

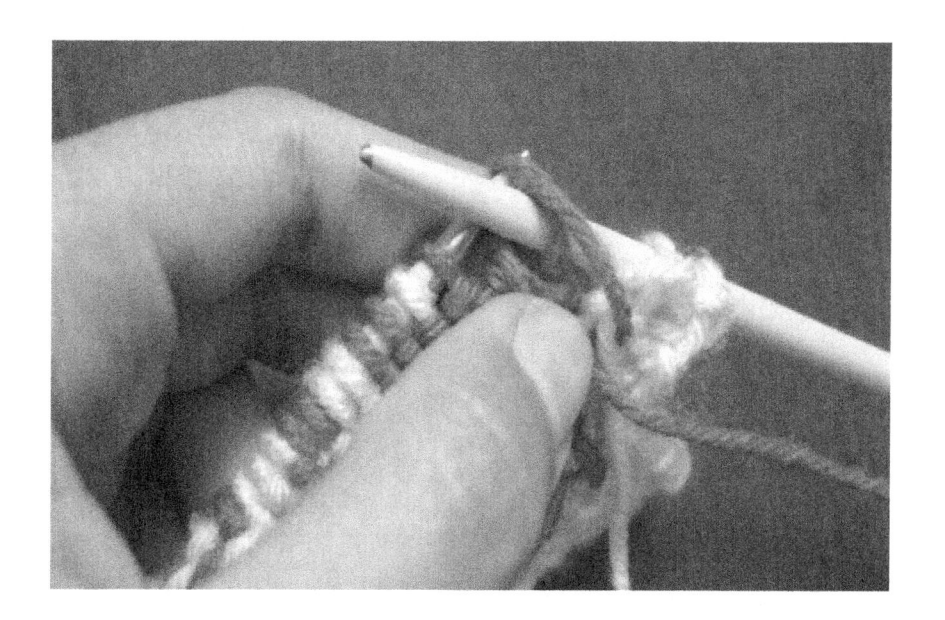

Cut yarn B. Tie the tail with the end to secure it then weave the end.

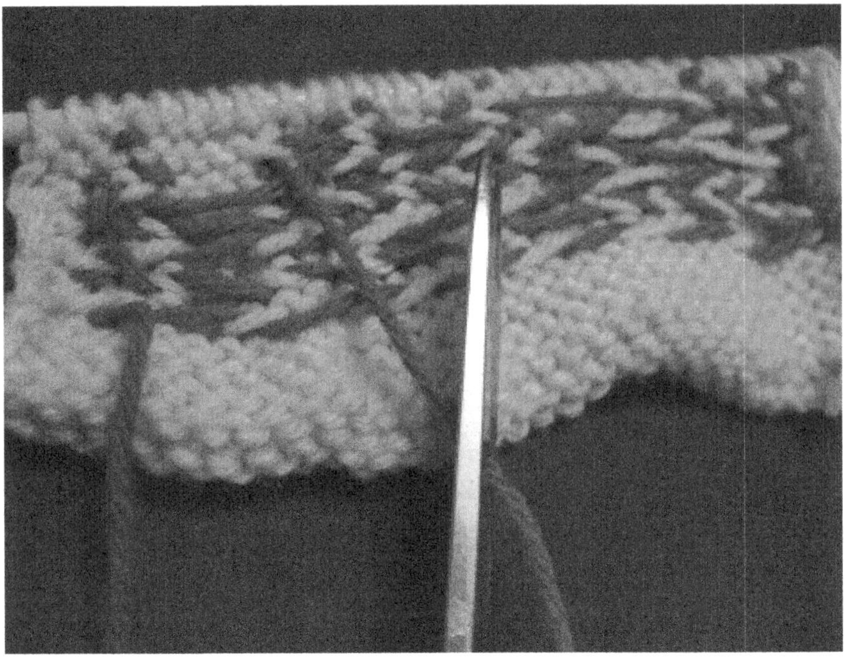

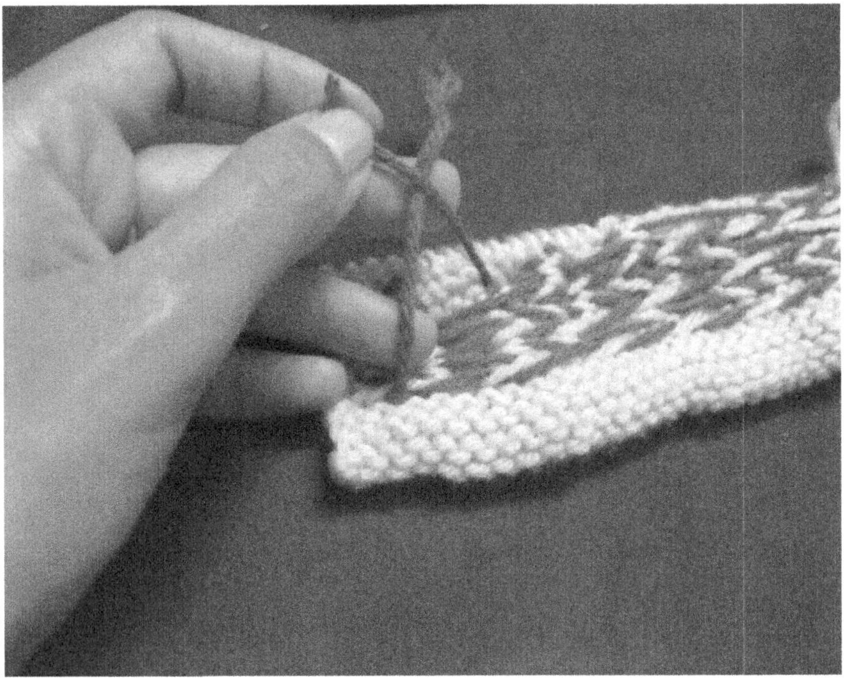

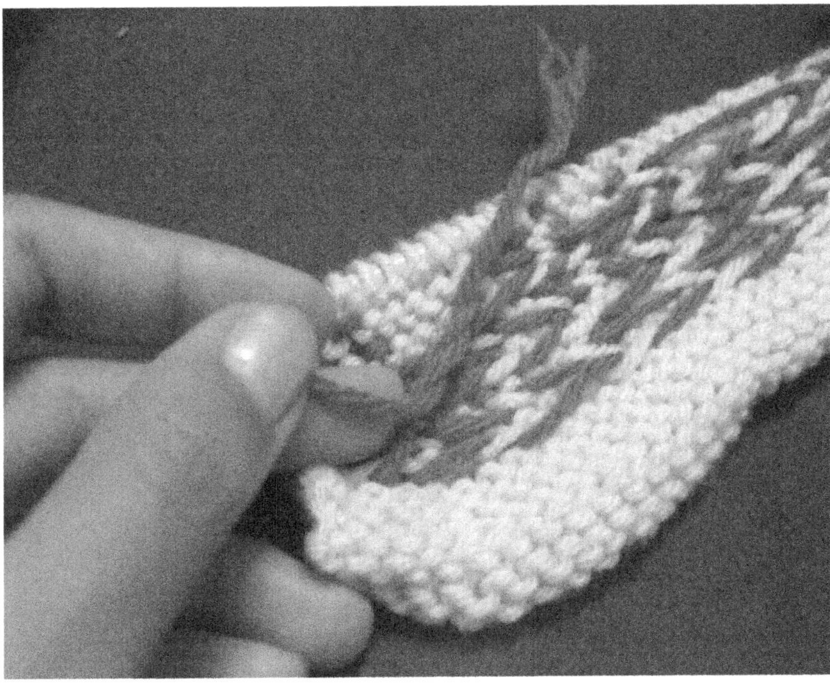

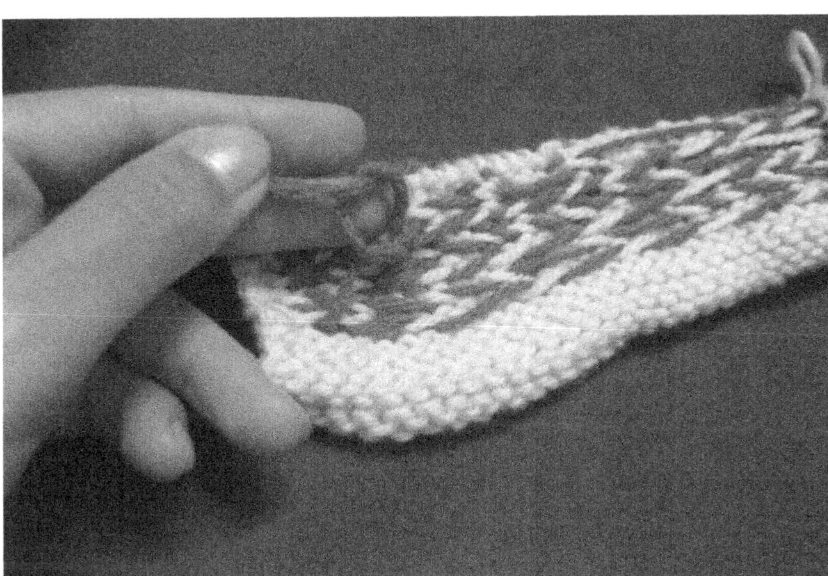

80

Here's an alphabet pattern that you may be able to use.

You can use these basic letters to make your own words and designs.

You can choose any pattern for the letters, and you can create your own unique pattern.

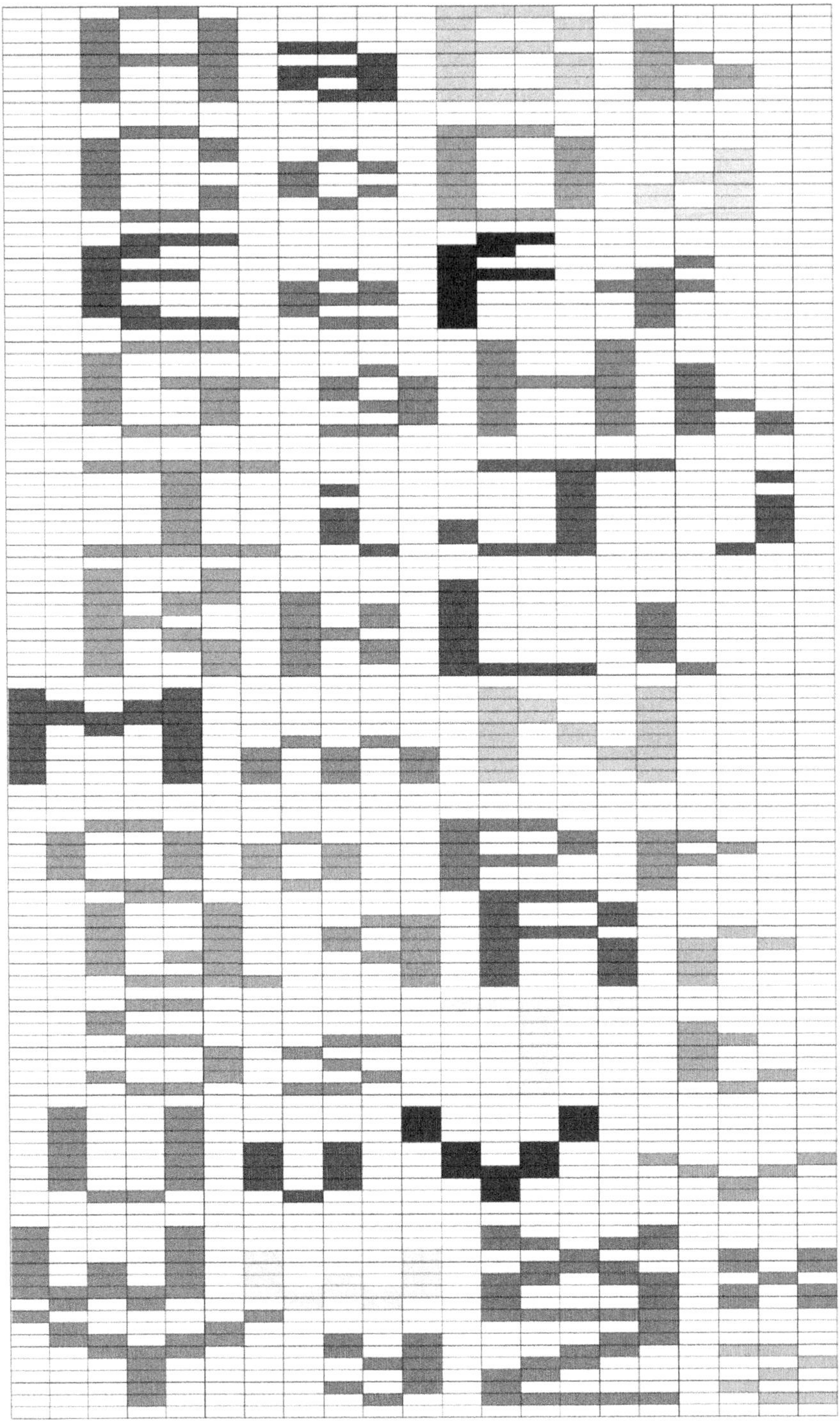

Drawing Shapes

Elephant Pattern

Let's create this adorable elephant! Draw it on a project using the stockinette stitch.

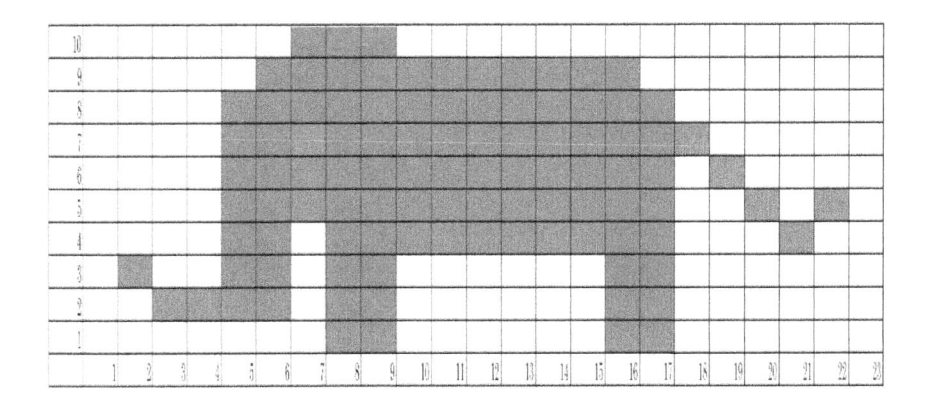

Choose color A for your work and color B for the elephant.

Knit 6 rows as a border and start from the seventh row to apply the pattern.

Read the chart from the bottom right-hand corner.

Row 1: The right side

- ❖ K6 with color A

- ❖ K2 by joining color B

- ❖ K6 with color A

- ❖ K2 with color B

- ❖ K7 with color A.

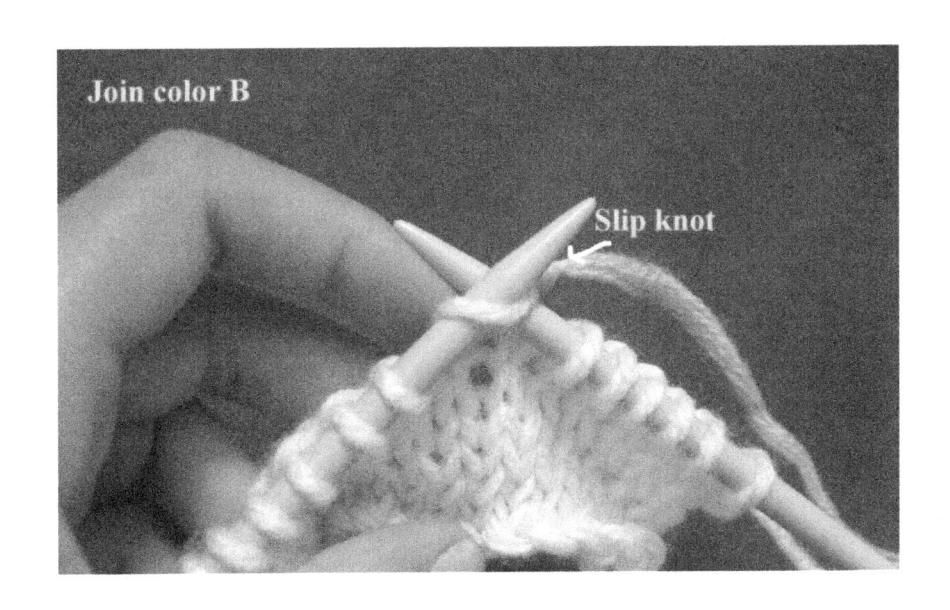

Row 2: The wrong side

- ❖ P2 with color A

- ❖ P4 with color B

- ❖ P1 with color A

- ❖ P2 with color B

- ❖ P6 with color A

- ❖ P2 with color B

- ❖ P6 with color A

Bring color A to the left and knit by color B

87

Row 3:

- ❖ K6 with color A
- ❖ K2 with color B
- ❖ K6 with color A
- ❖ K2 with color B
- ❖ K1 with color A
- ❖ K4 with color B

❖ K2 with color A

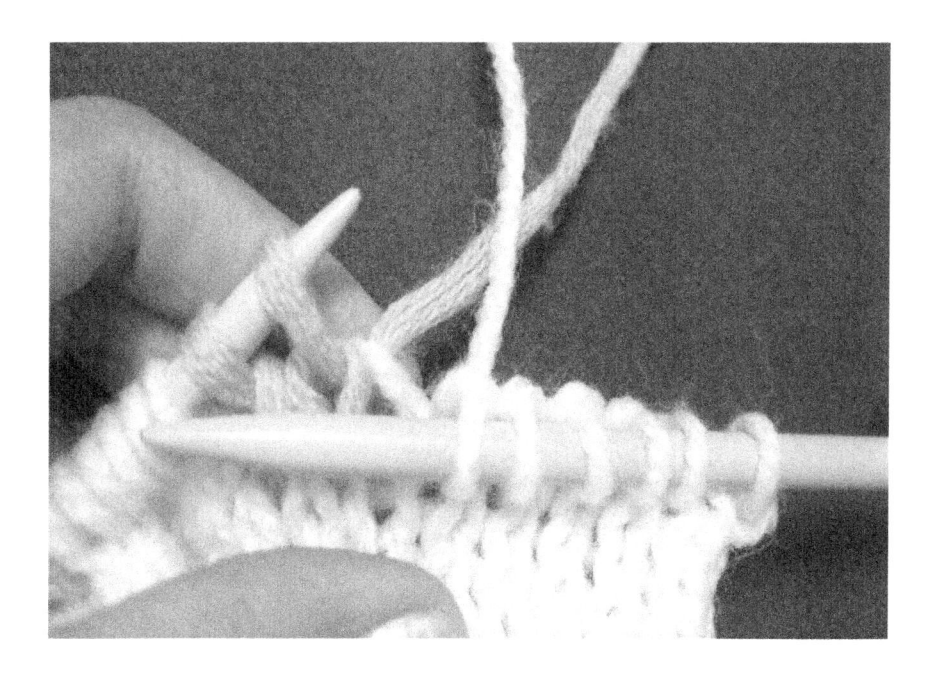

Row 4:

- ❖ P4 with color A

- ❖ P2 with color B

- ❖ P1 with color A

- ❖ P10 with color B

- ❖ P3 with color A

- ❖ P1 with color B

- ❖ P2 with color A

Row 5:

- ❖ K1 with color A

- ❖ K1 with color B

- ❖ K1 with color A

- ❖ K1 with color B

- ❖ K2 with color A

- ❖ K13 with color B

- ❖ K4 with color A.

Row 6:

- P4 with color A

- P13 with color B

- P1 with color A

- P1 with color B

- P4 with color A

Row 7:

- K5 with color A

- K11 with color B

- K1 with color C

- K2 with color B

- K4 with color A

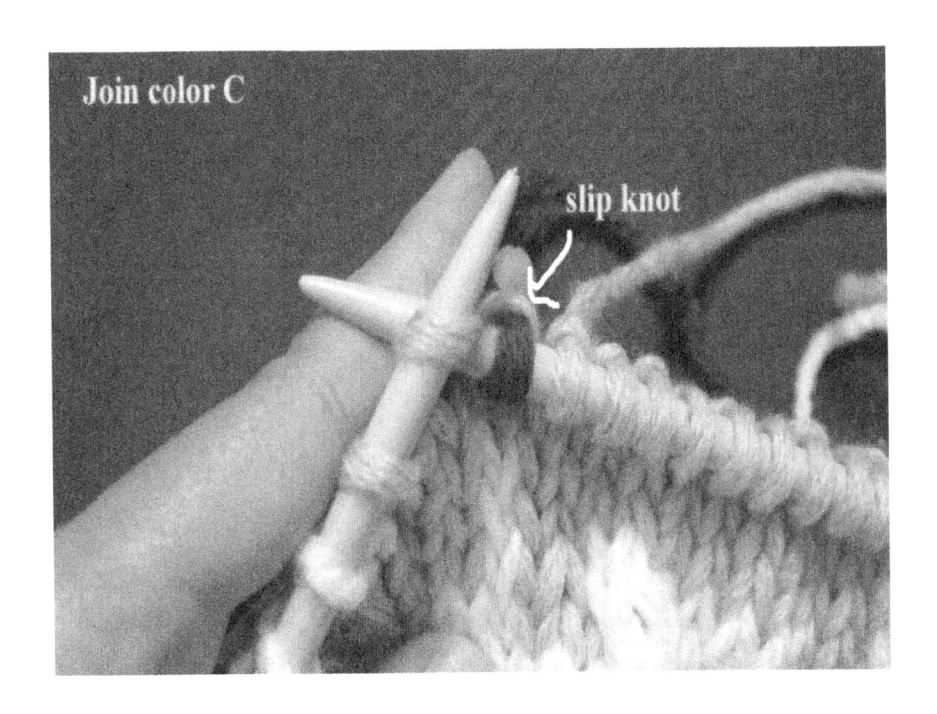

Row 8:

- ❖ P4 with color A
- ❖ P13 with color B
- ❖ K6 with color A

Row 9:

- K7 with color A

- K11 with color B

- K5 with color A

Row 10:

- P6 with color A

- P3 with color B

- ❖ K14 with color A

After you have finished the pattern, you can cut the yarn end and tie them together. Weave in the loose ends.

FREE BONUS PATTERNS

Jacquard means having a repeated decorative drawing on knitting like these patterns.

It is an intricately woven pattern.

The only limit is your imagination!

You can make nearly everything with Jacquard knitting.

If you don't see a pattern in this list of over 20 patterns, you can create your own using graph paper.

You will see some examples in this group of patterns.

You can download these patterns to print them yourself at this link: https://tinyurl.com/FavoriteKnitPatterns

Winter Flower 1

Winter Flower 2

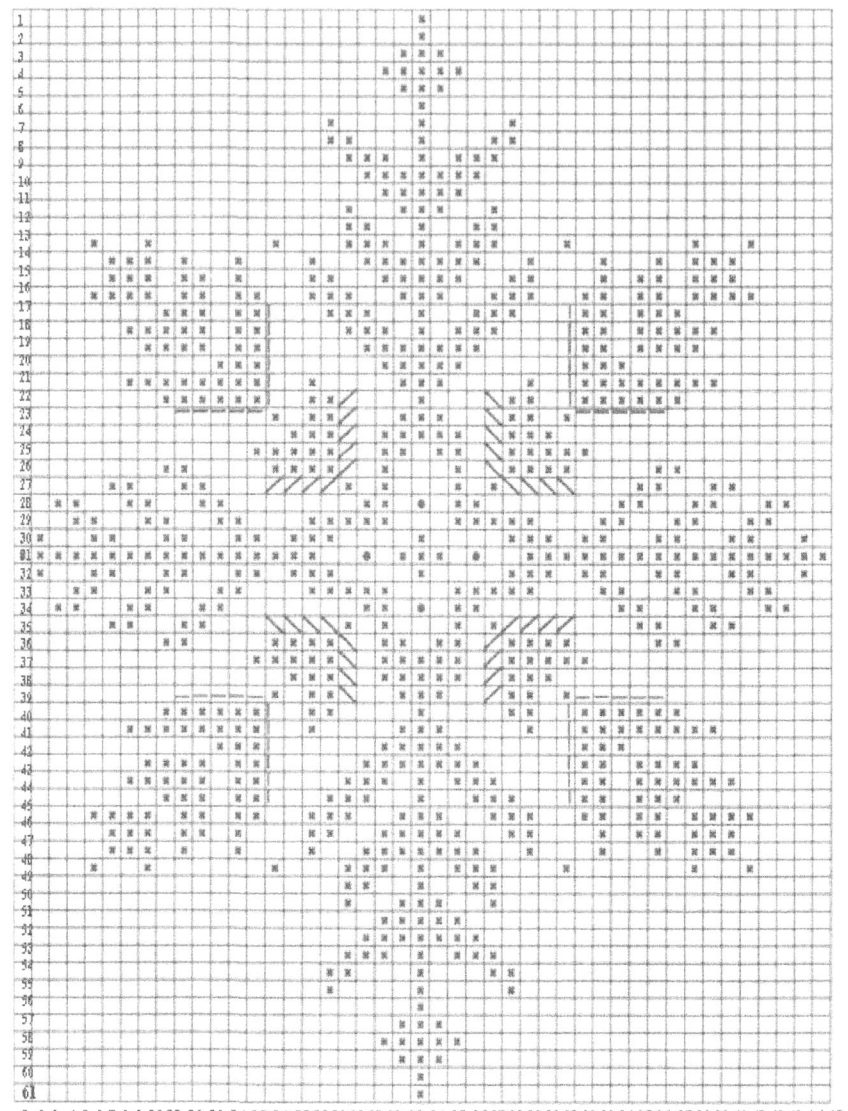

100

Reindeer

Christmas Tree

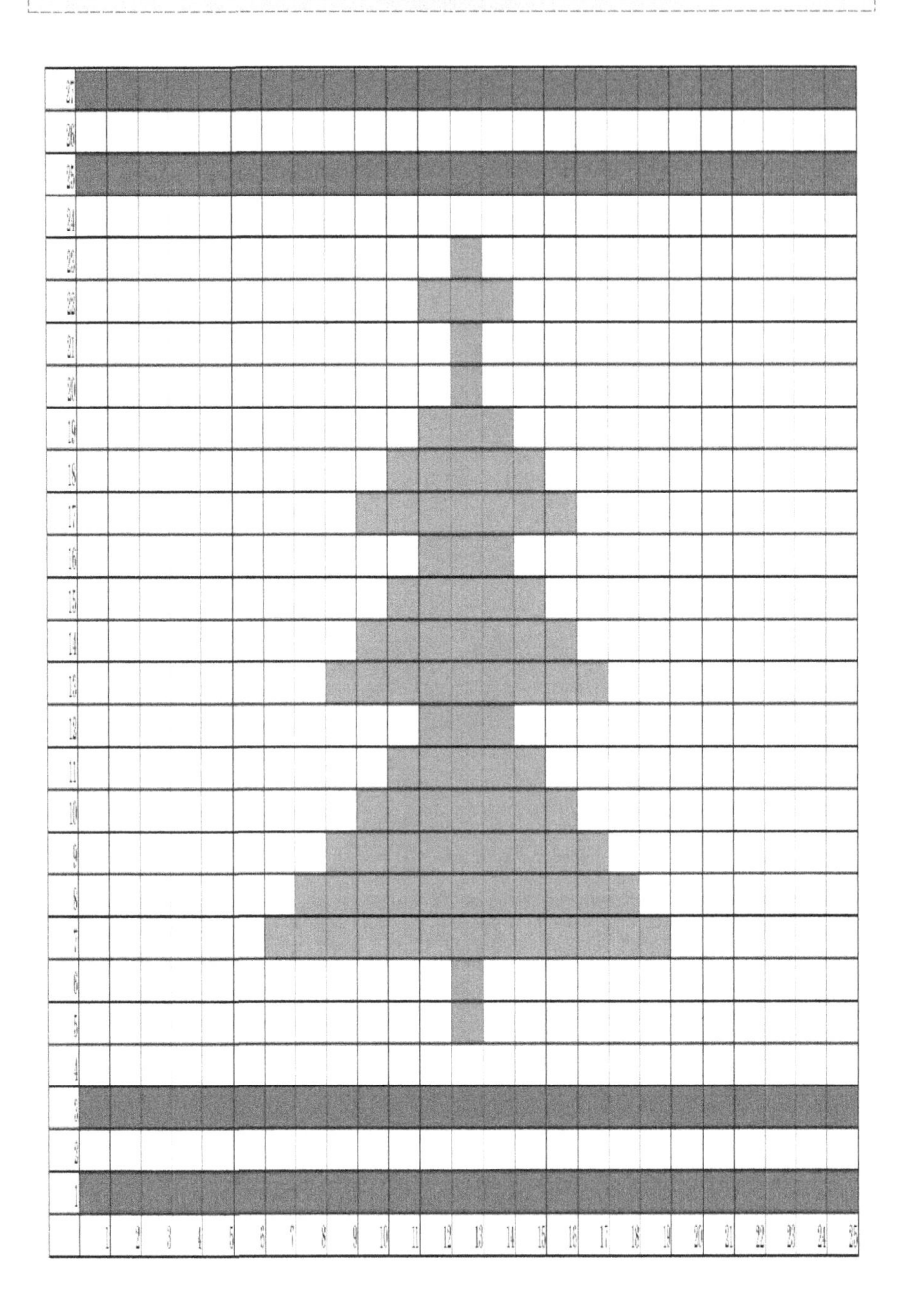

Reindeer and Tree

Hand-Drawn Reindeer

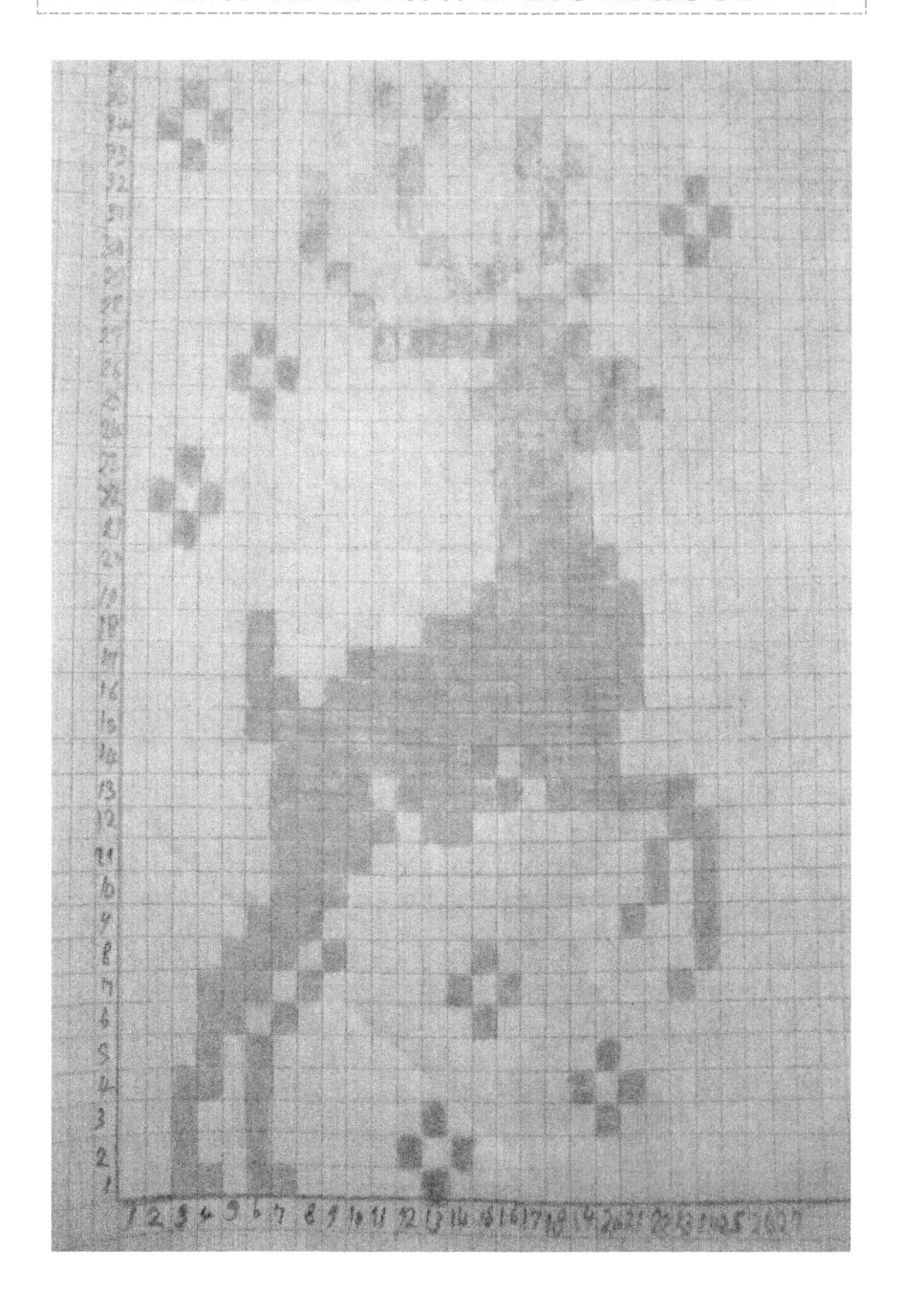

Freeform

Tiger Decorative

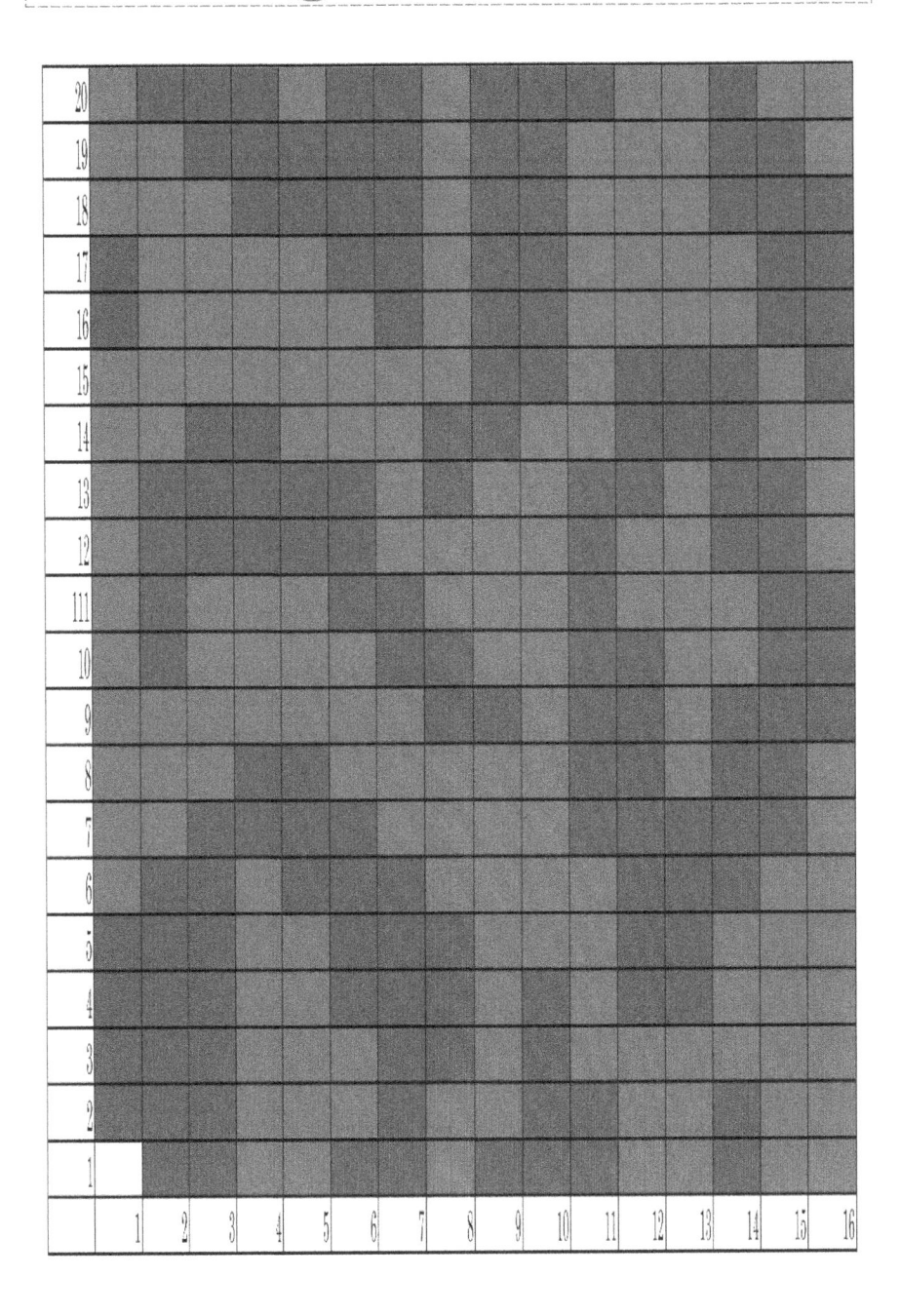

Butterfly

Heart

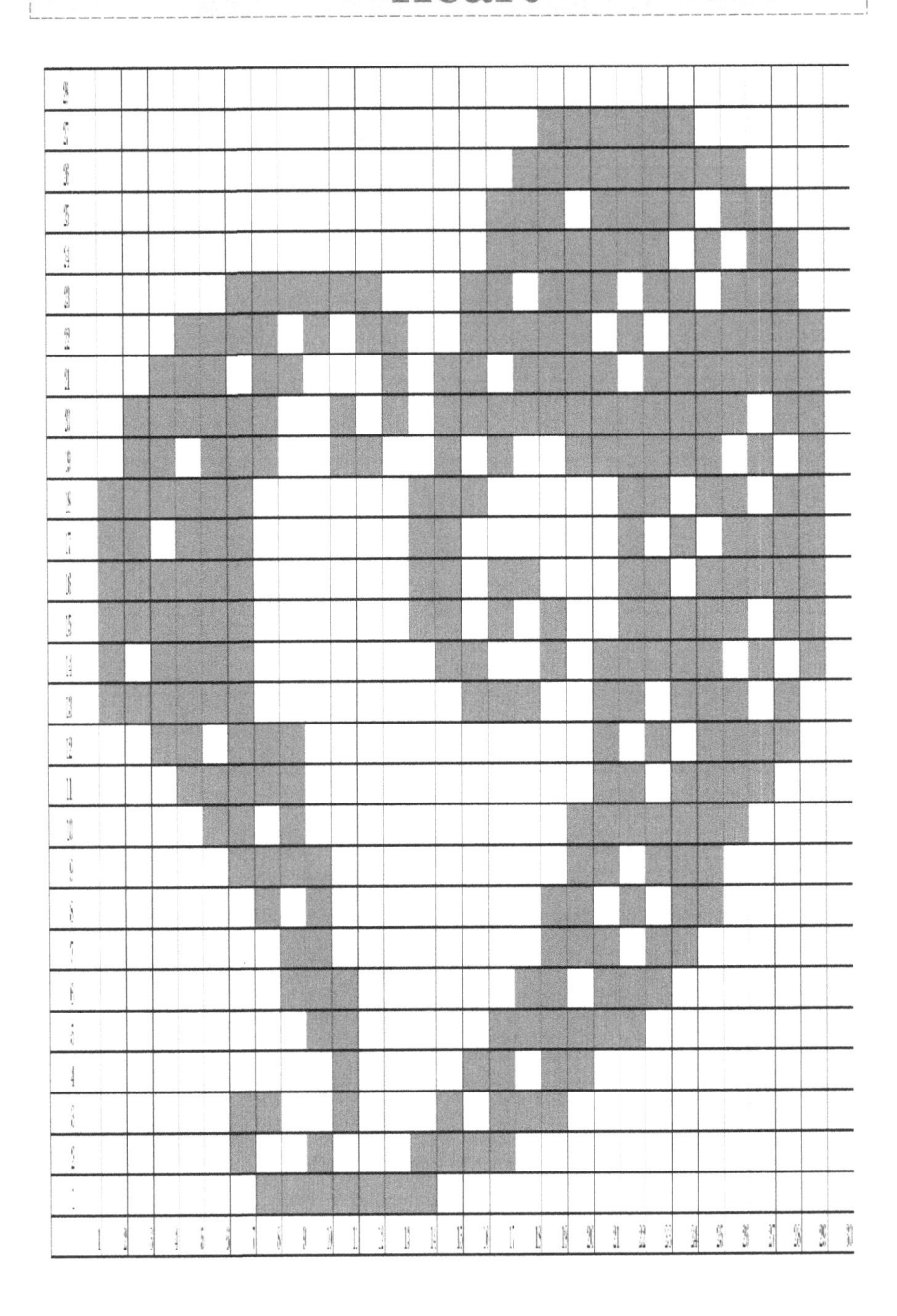

Mouse

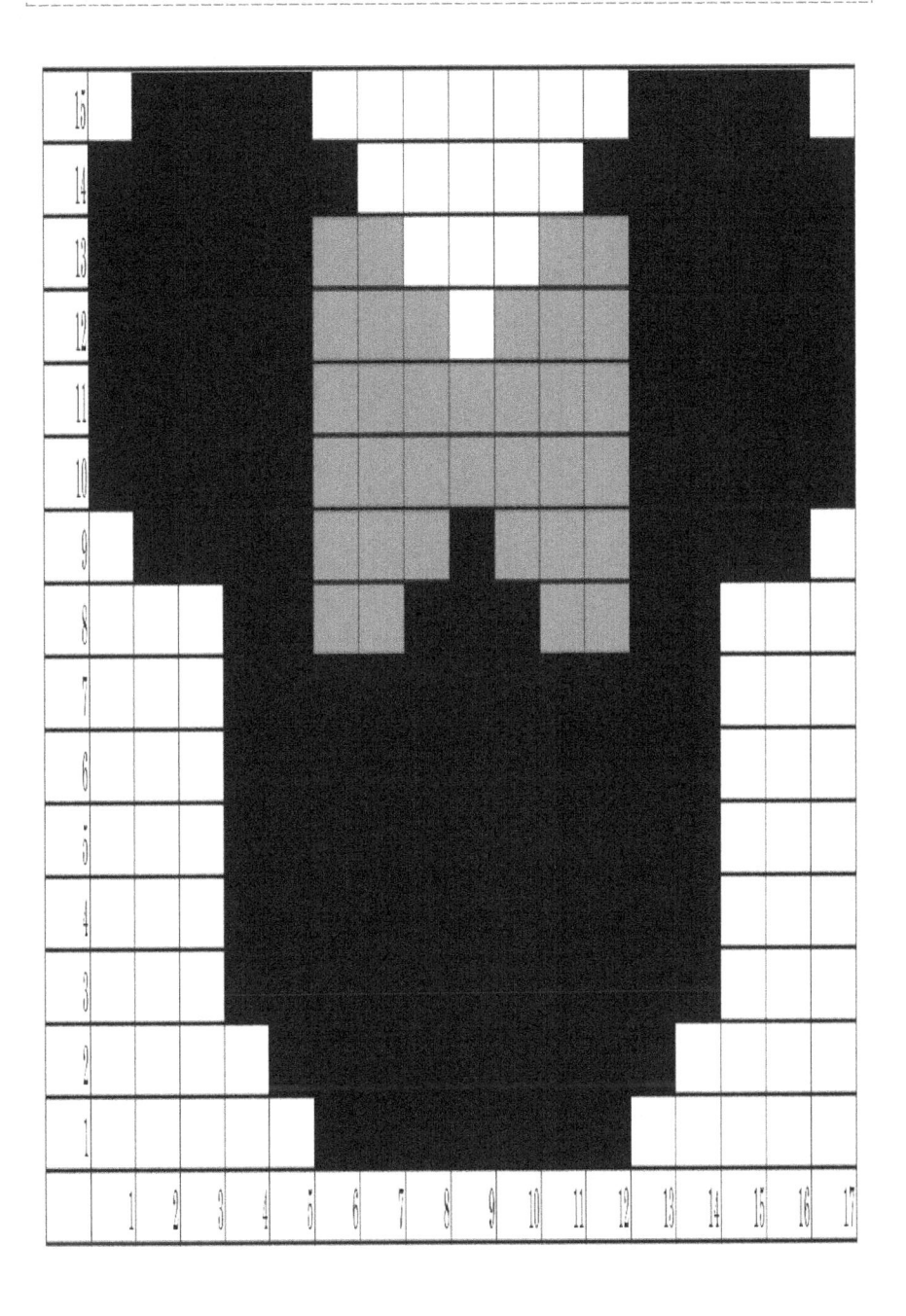

Owl

Strawberry

Dog

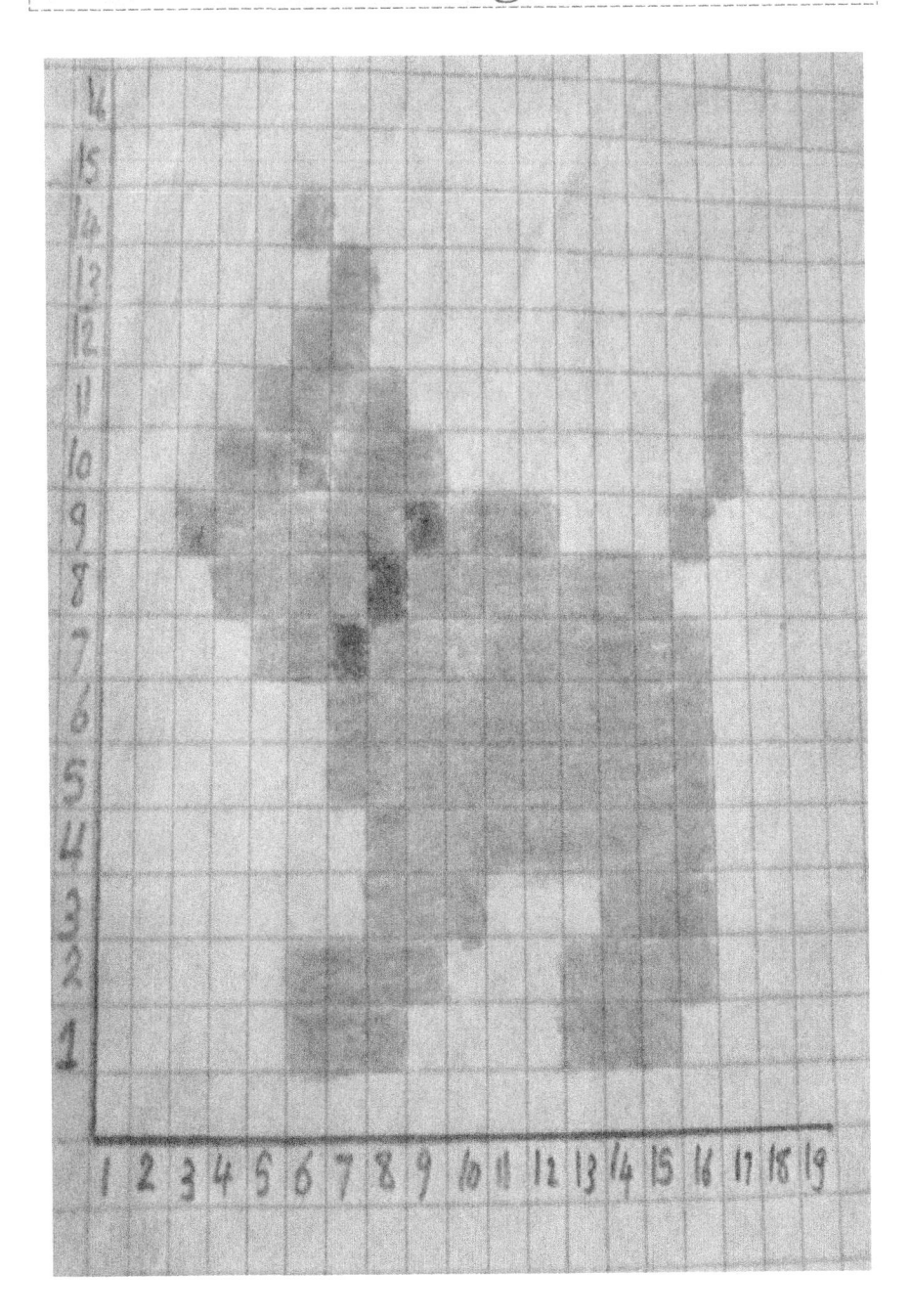

Rabbit

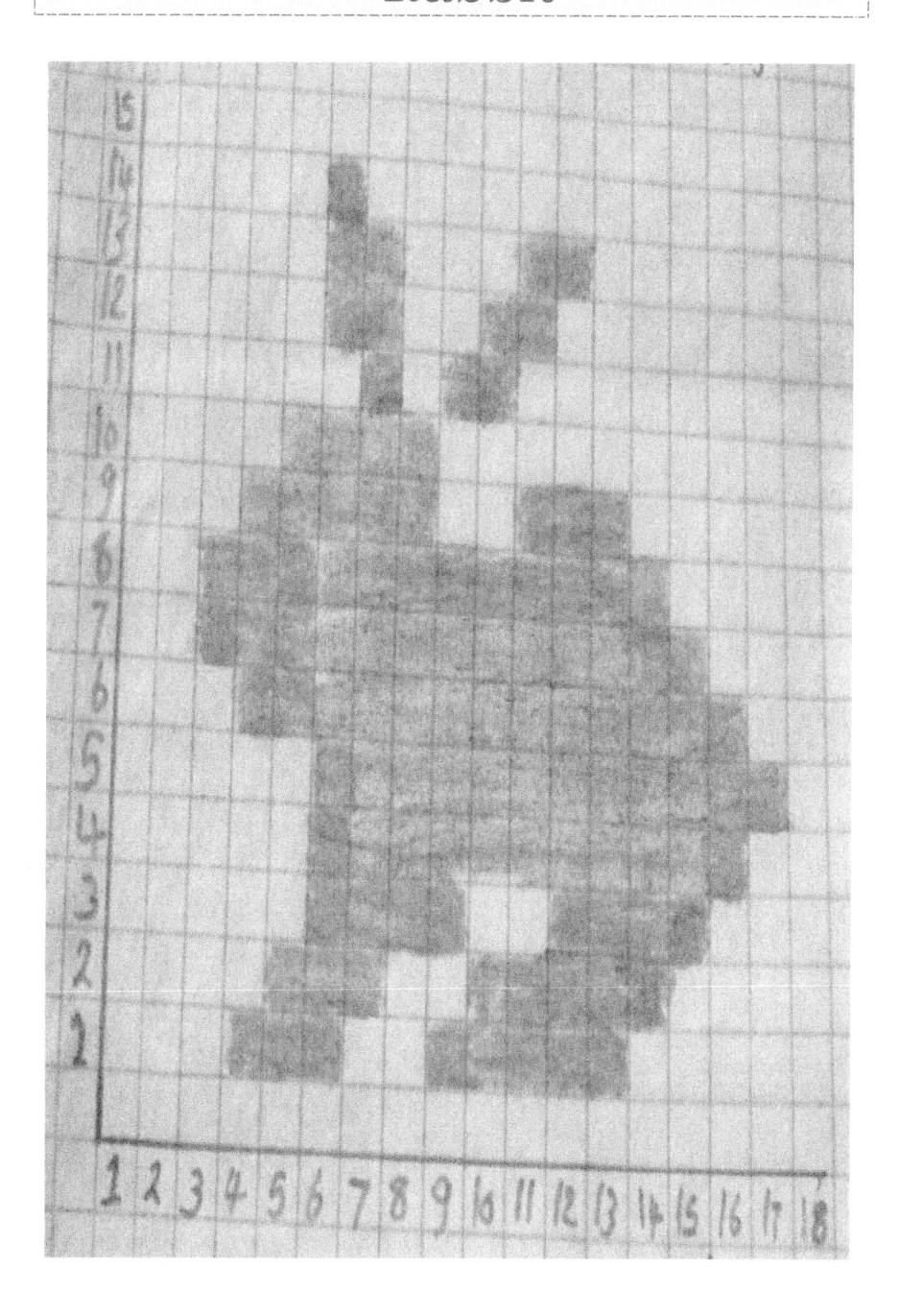

Swan

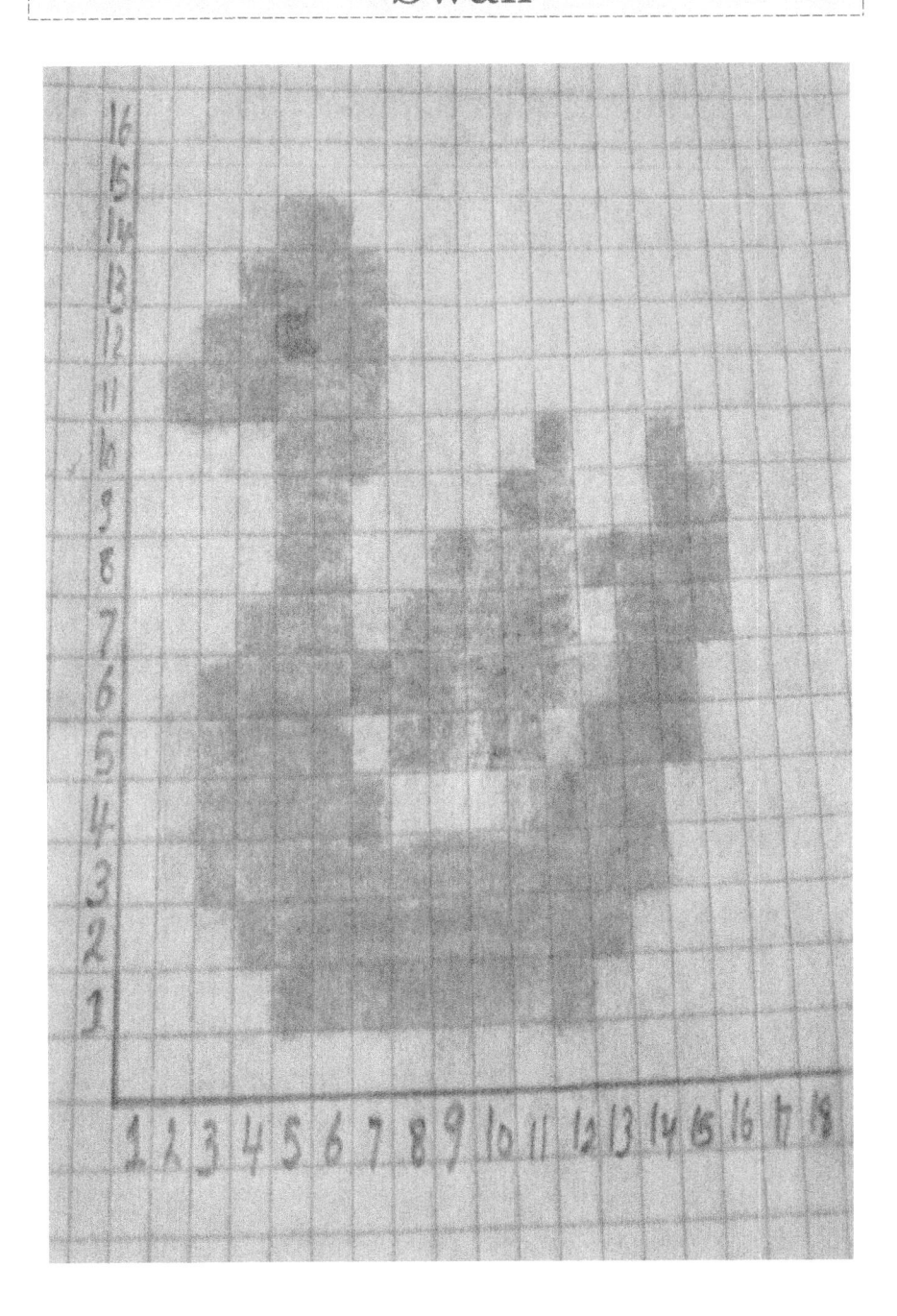

Cat

Ancient Egyptian Beetle

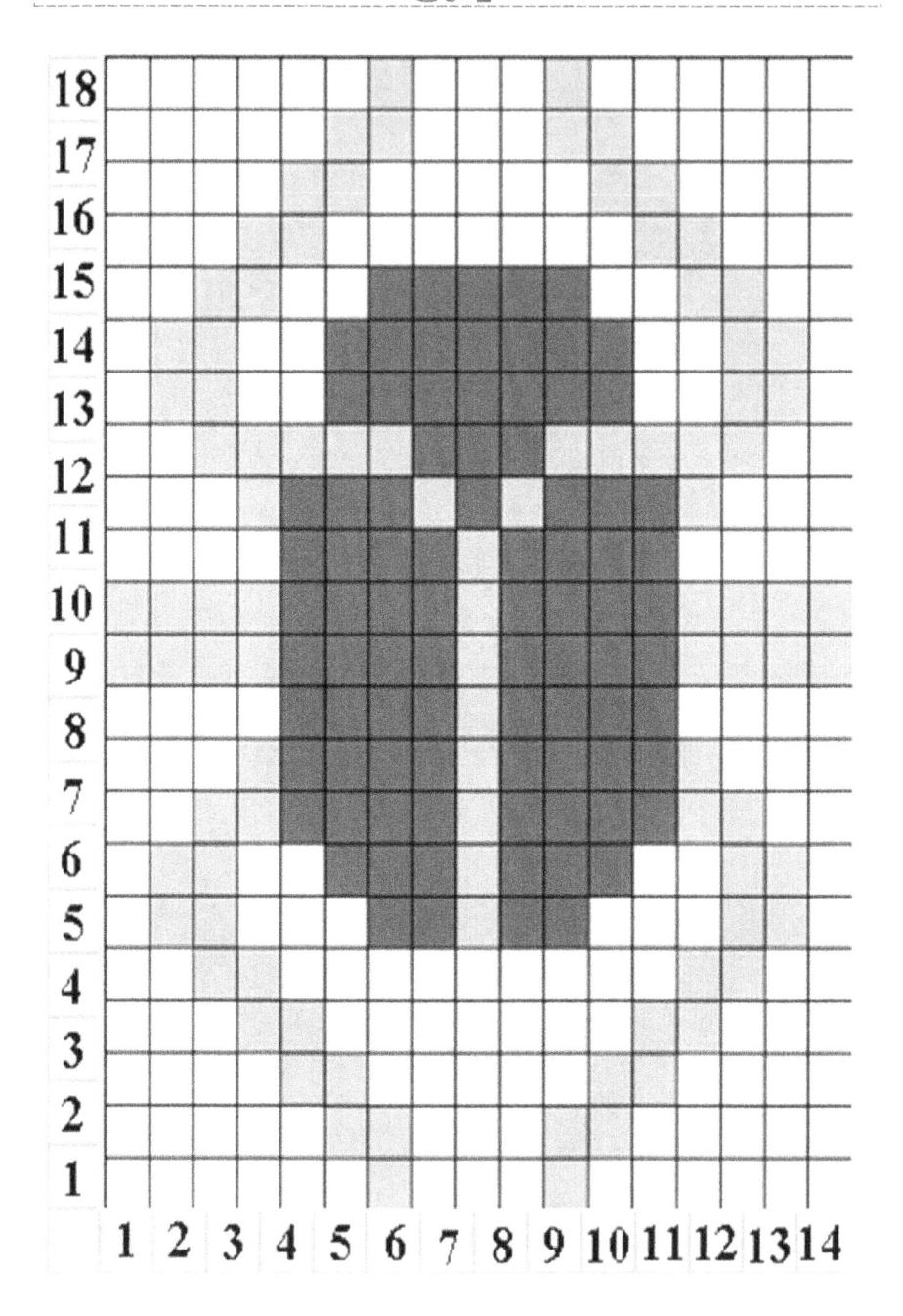

Nefertiti Queen

Sphinx

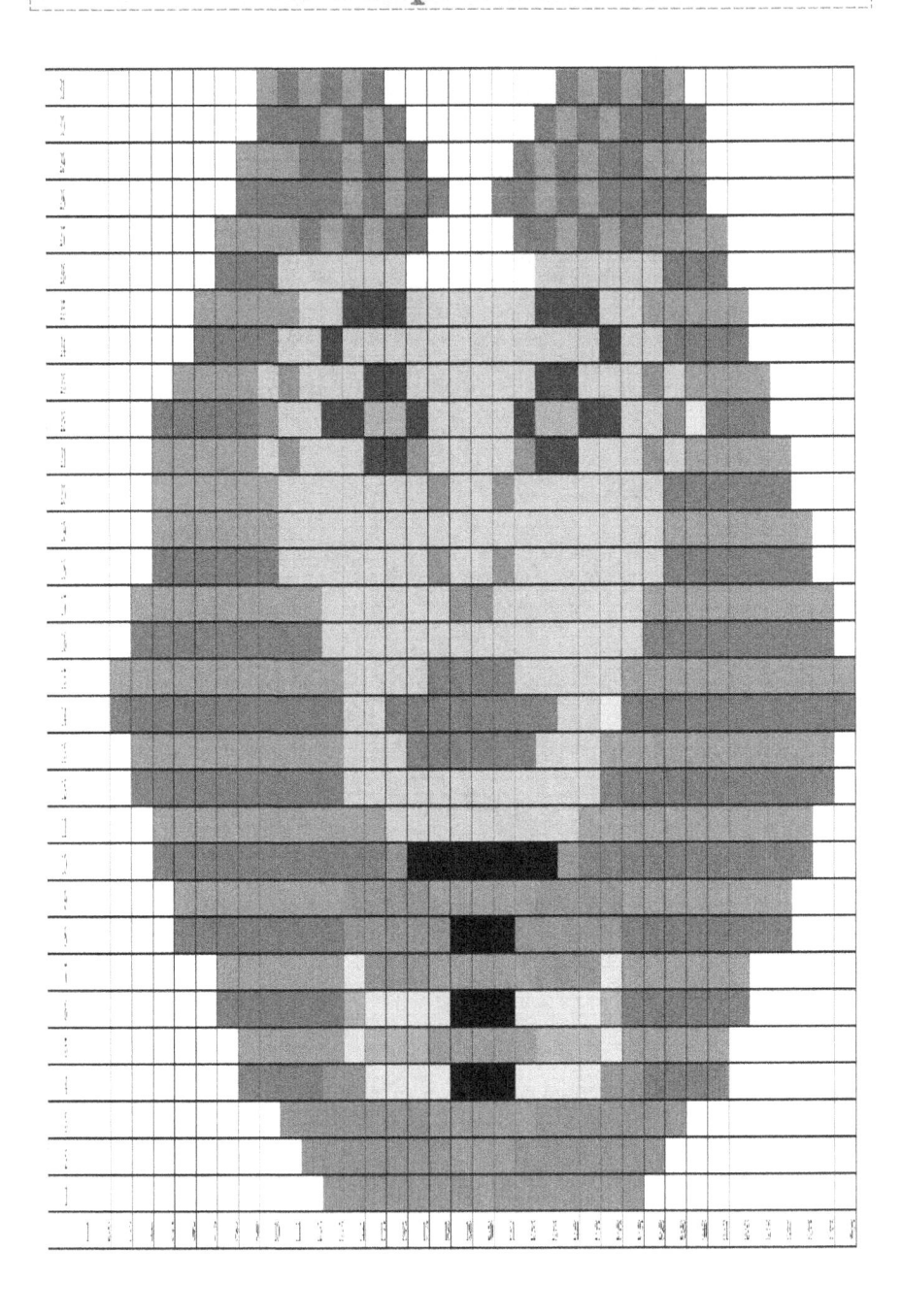

Ancient Egyptian Eye

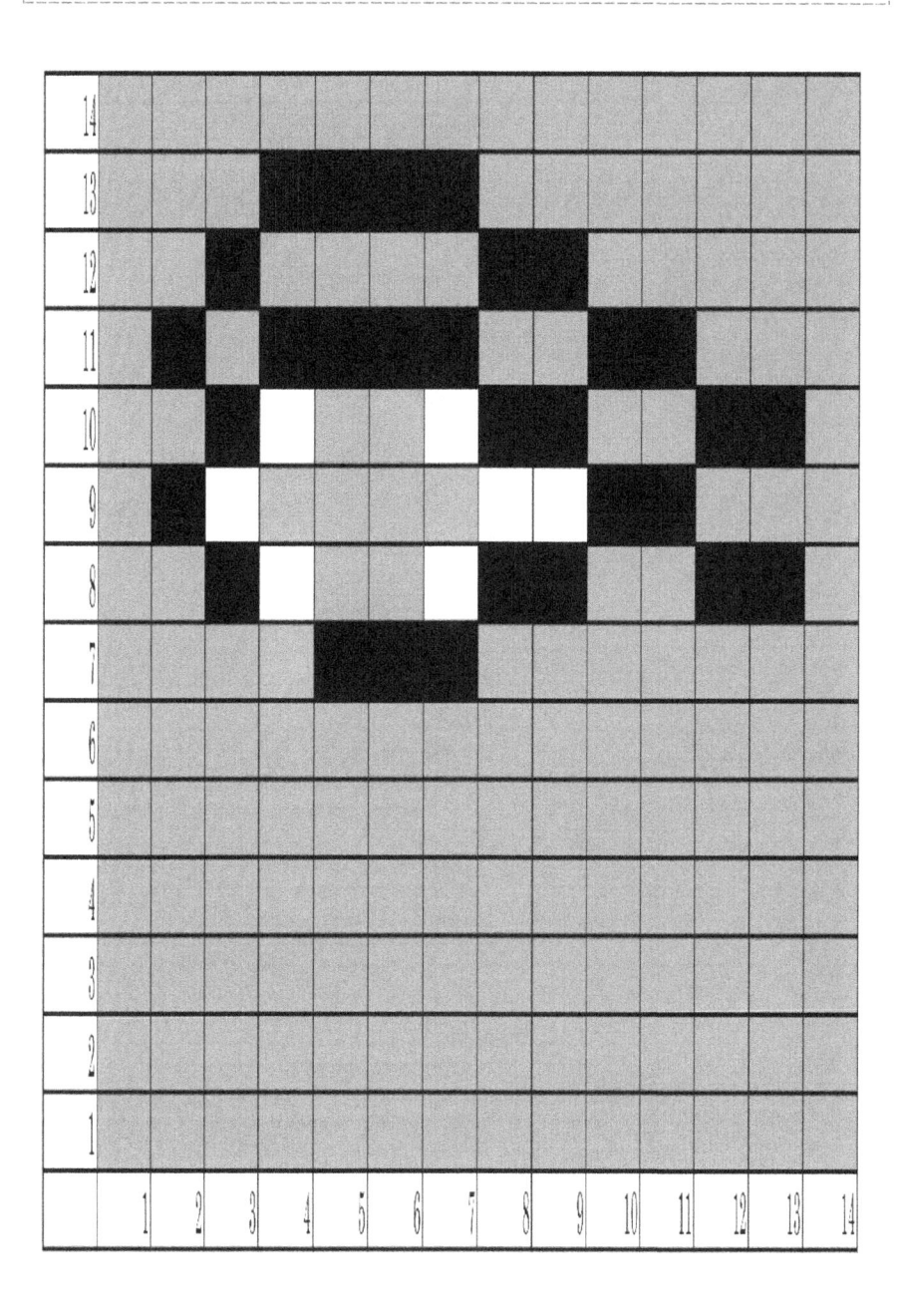

Egyptian Ankh

Lace Stitches

Lace knitting is a style of knitting characterized by stable "holes" in the fabric arranged with consideration of aesthetic value.

There are many varied methods of creating lace stitches. They all have different outcomes.

Drop Stitch (The Horizontal River)

This stitch is amazing for spring and summer scarfs.

Cast on any number of stitches.

Row 1: Knit all the stitches.

Row 2: Knit all the stitches.

Row 3: Knit all the stitches.

Row 4: K1. [YO2x (wrap the yarn around the right needle 2 times), K1] repeat until the end of the row.

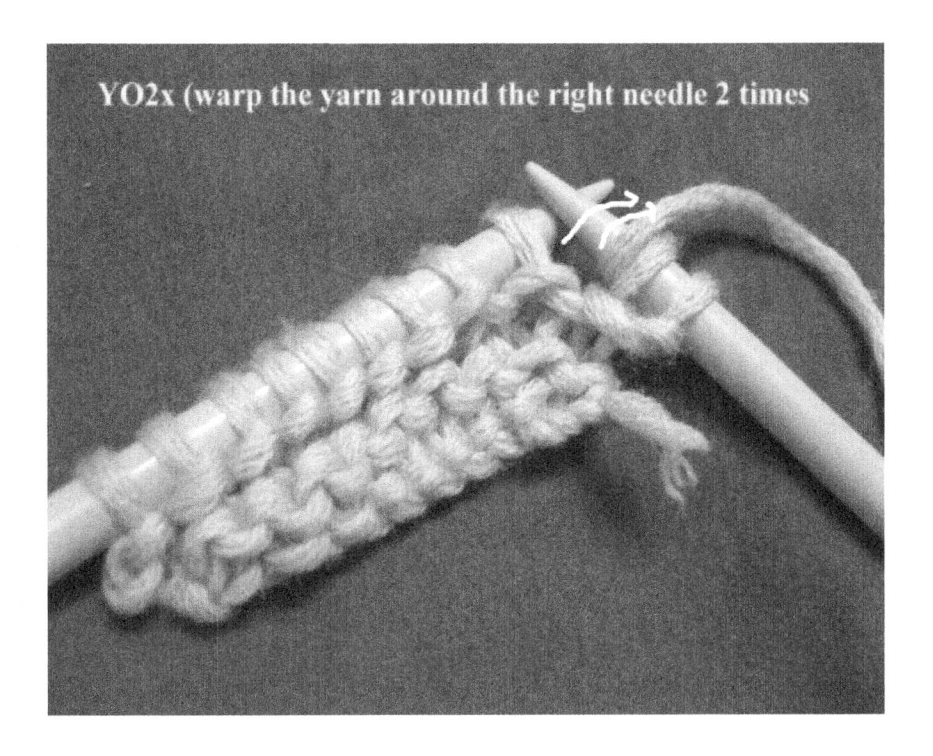

Row 5: Knit the original stitches and drop the YO.

Drop the YO

drop the YO

drop the YO

Repeat from the first row.

Horizontal River, Alternative Method

There is another way to do a drop/horizontal river stitch.

Rows 1-4: Knit these rows.

Rows 4 and 5: Insert your right needle into the first stitch. Wrap the yarn around the two needles. Put it between the two needles. Knit the stitch. Repeat until the end of the row.

Put the yarn between the two needles and knit the stitch

Continue doing this repeating from the first row.

The Vertical River

Cast on a number of stitches that can be divided by 4. Add 2 for the edges.

Row 1: K1, (K2, YO, SKP) "SKP" means slip1, k1, pass slipped stitch over. Repeat until the last stitch. Knit it (K1).

Row 2: K1, (P2, YO, P2tog) repeat until the last stitch. Knit it (K1).

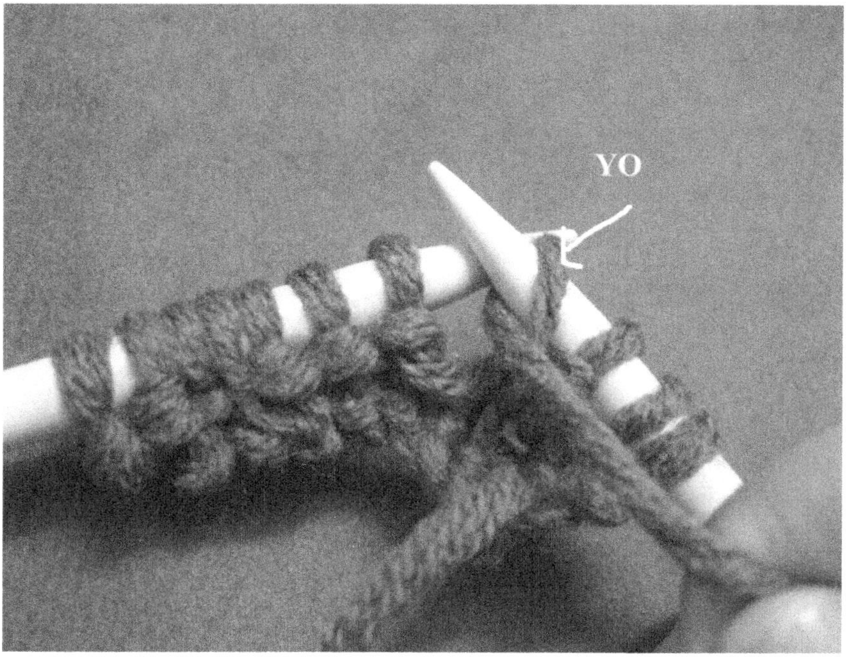
YO

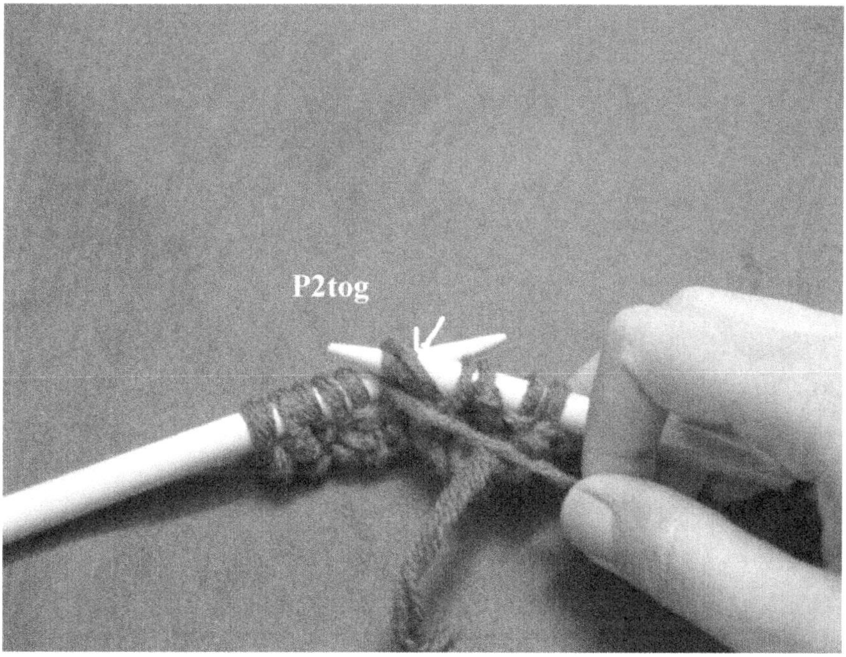
P2tog

Repeat from the first row.

Herringbone Lace Rib Stitch

Cast on a number of stitches that can be divided by 7. Add 1.

Row 1: K1, (p1, k1, YO, P2tog, K1, P1, K1)

Row 2: P1, (K2, YO, P2tog, K2, P1). Create subsequent rows by repeating this pattern.

Simple Lace

Cast on a number of stitches that can be divided by 4. Add 2.

Row 1: K1, (YO, SKP, K2) repeat until the last stitch, knit it (K1).

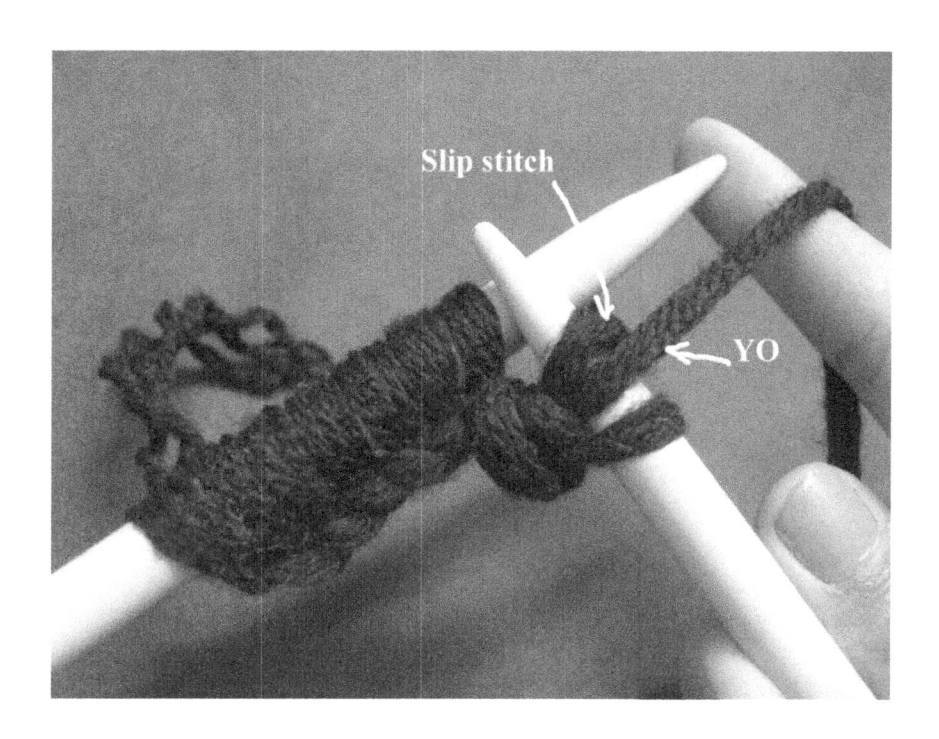

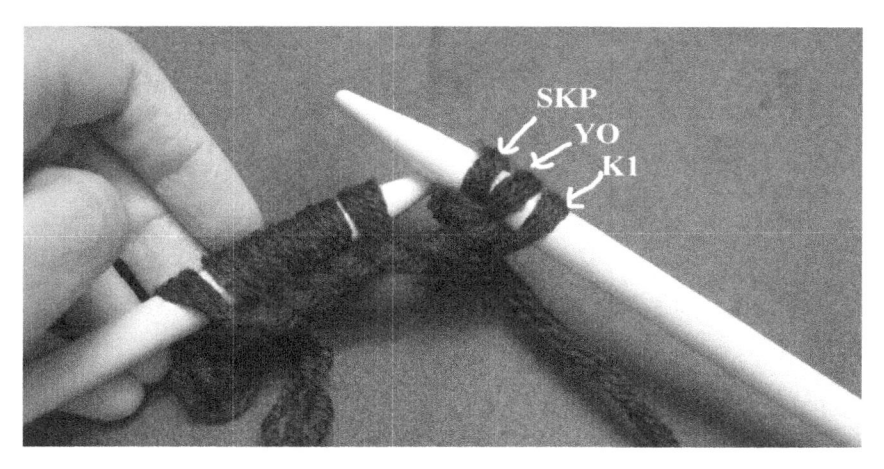

Row 2: Purl all the stitches.

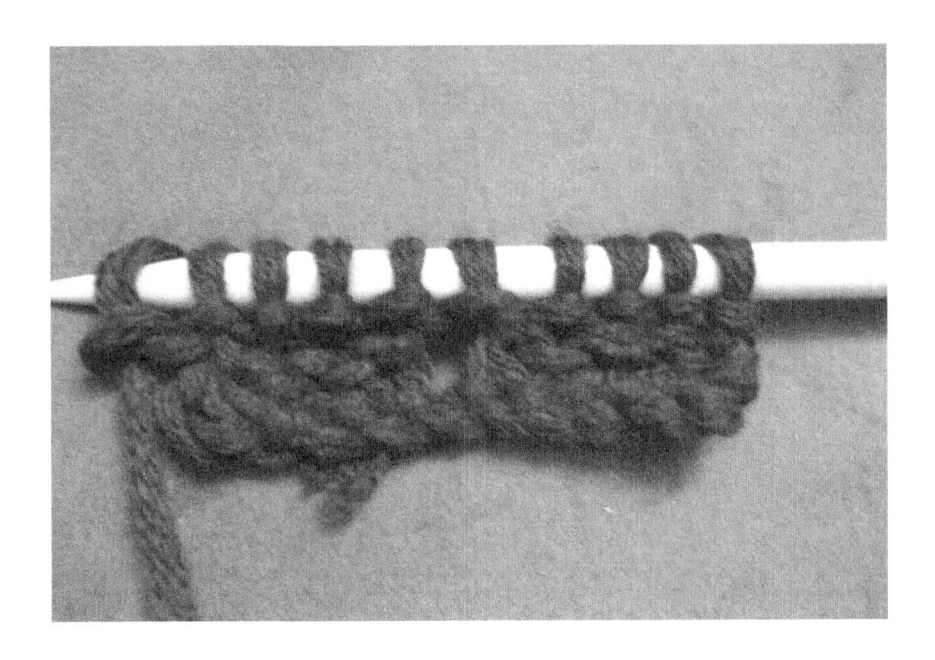

Row 3: Knit all the stitches.

Row 4: Purl all the stitches.

Row 5: K1, (K2, YO, SKP) When you get to the last stitch, K1.

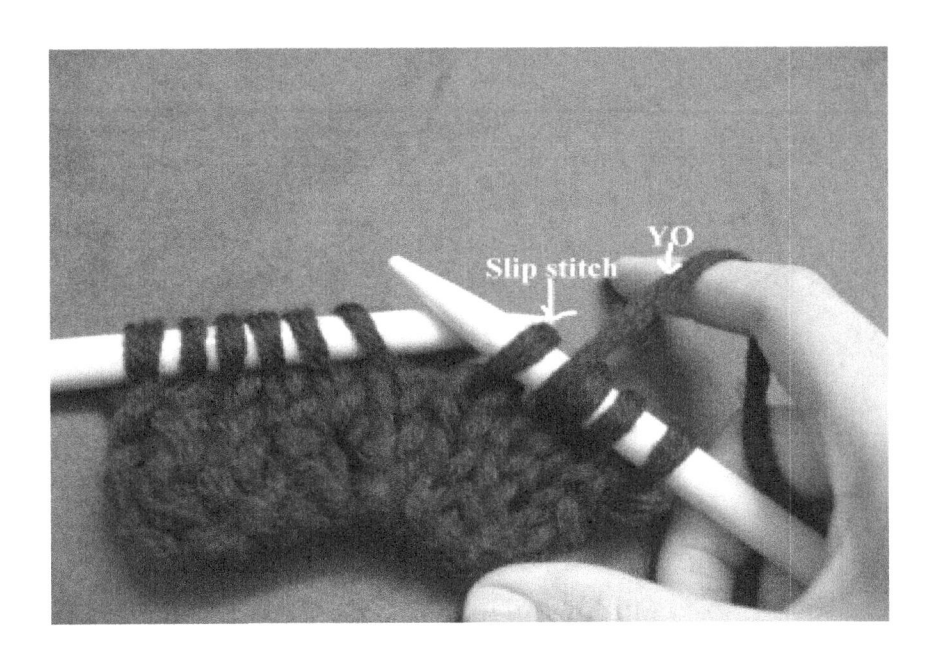

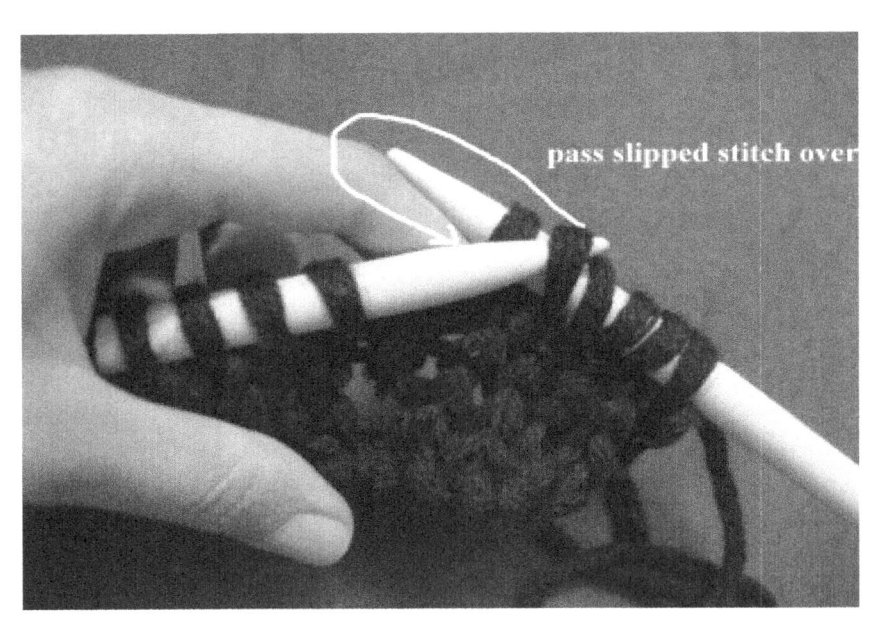

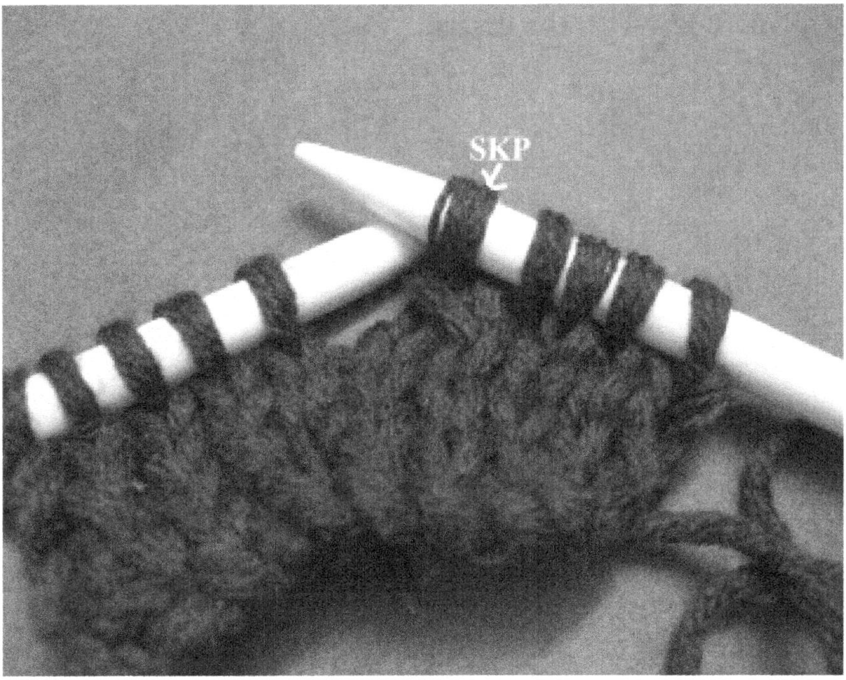
SKP

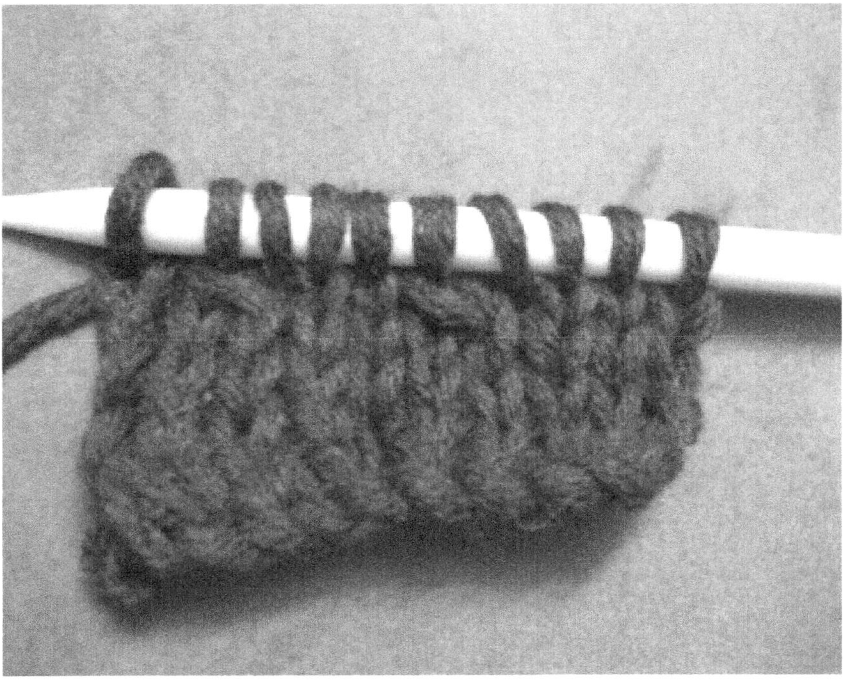

Row 6: Purl all the stitches.

Row 7: Knit all the stitches.

Row 8: Purl all the stitches.

Spider Web Lace

Cast on a number of stitches that can be divided by 4. Add 2.

Row 1: K1, [KPK (knit, purl and knit into the same stitch), P3tog] repeat until the last stitch, knit it (K1).

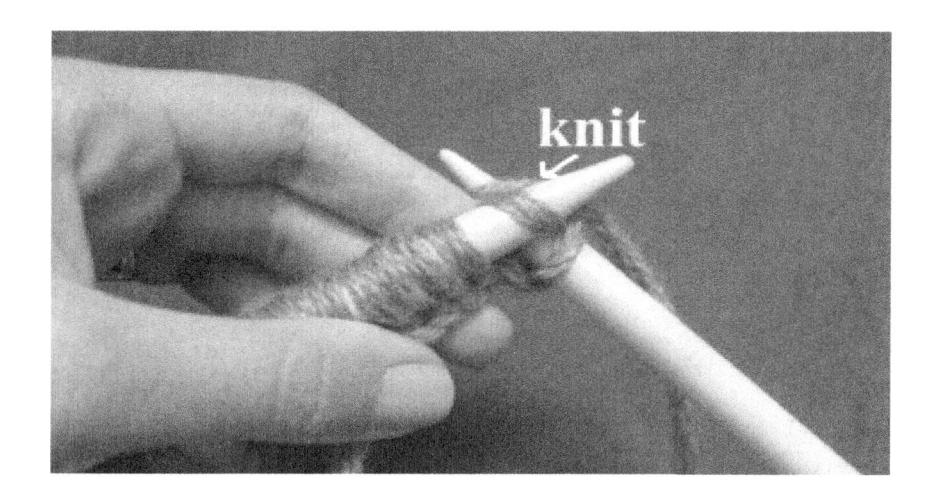

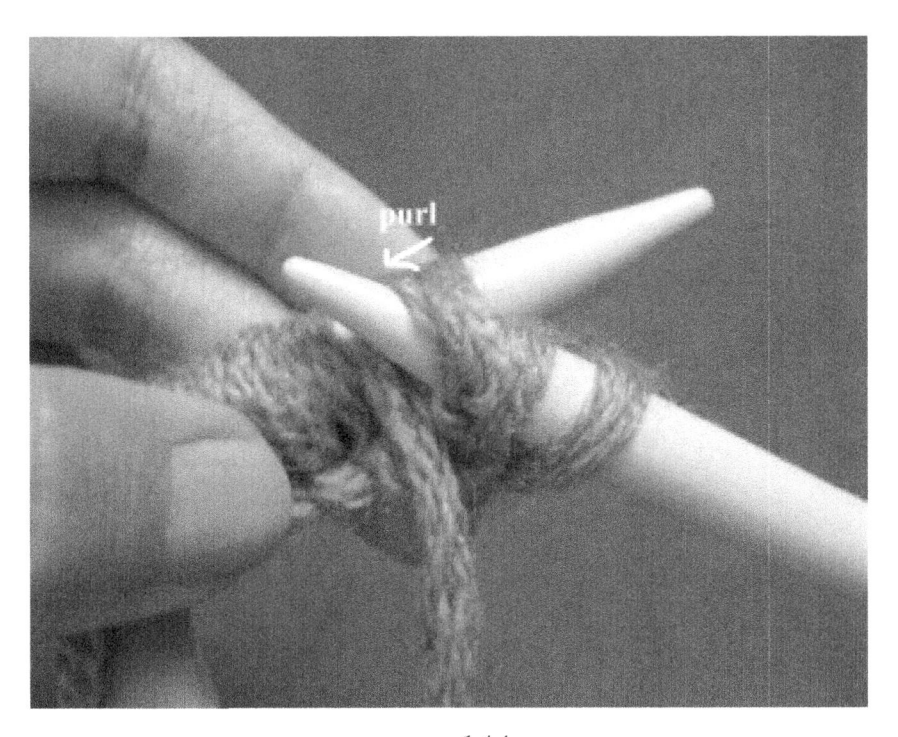

bring the yarn to the front and purl into the same stitch

purl

Don't slip the stitch and put the yarn in the back

knit the stitch

knit the stitch

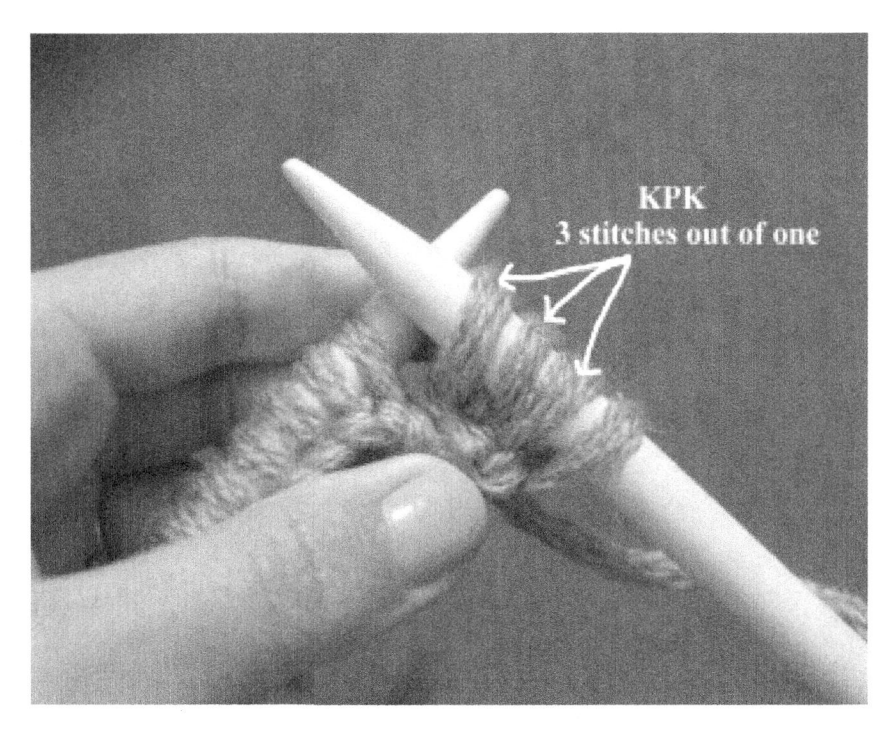

KPK
3 stitches out of one

P3tog

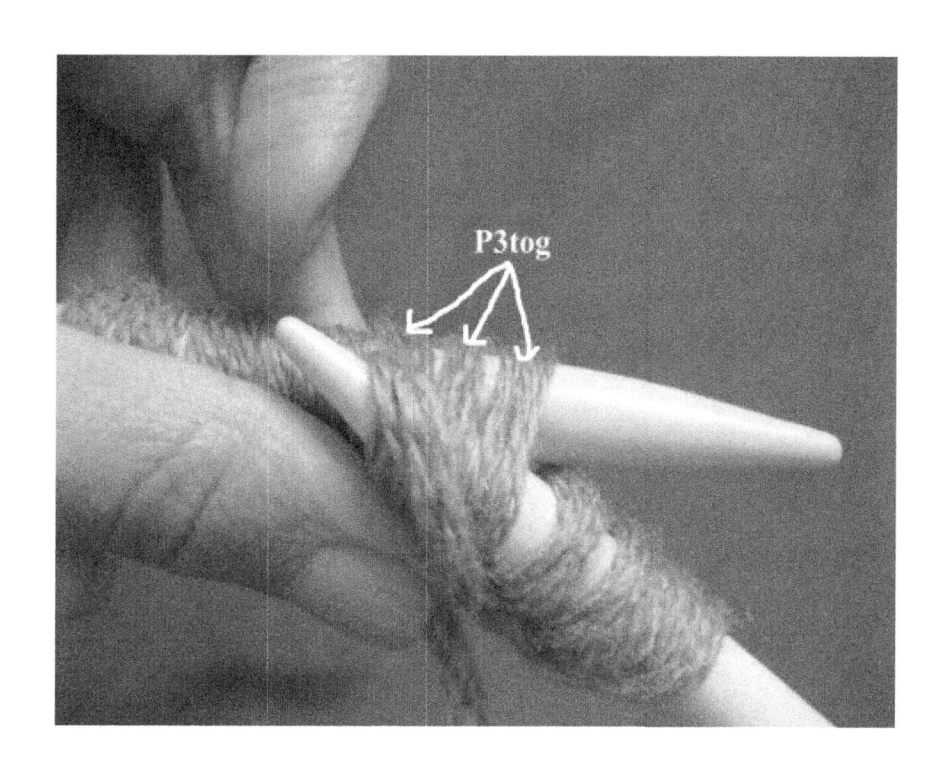

Row 2: Purl all the stitches.

Row 3: K1, (K3tog, KPK) repeat until the last stitch, knit it (K1)

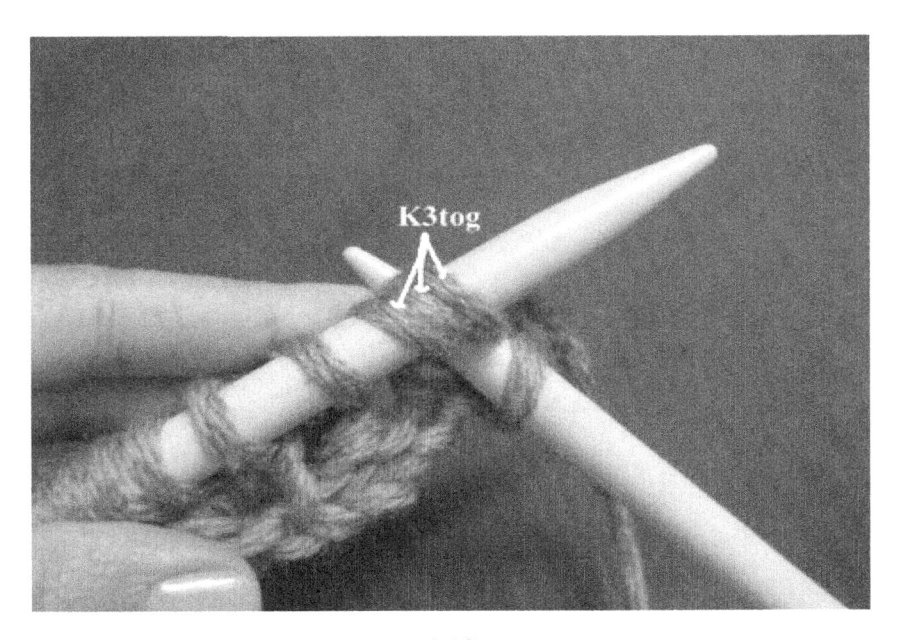

Knit and don't slip the stitch

purl and don't slip the stitch

knit the stitch

KPK 3 stitches out of one

Row 4: Purl all the stitches. Note that you can consider the wrong side of the stitch as the front side.

Turkish Lace Stitch

Cast on an even number of stitches. Add 2 for the edges.

Every Row: K1, (YO, SKP) repeat what is in parenthesis until the last stitch. Knit the last stitch in the row (K1).

Continue this until you reach the desired length.

Broken Lace Stitch

Cast on a number of stitches that can be divided by 7. Add 2.

Row 1: K1, (K5, K2tog, YO) to the last stitch, knit it (K1).

Row 2: Purl all the stitches.

Row 3: K1, (K4, K2tog, YO, K1) Repeat until the last stitch, knit it (K1).

Row 4: Purl all the stitches.

Row 5: K1, (K3, K2tog, YO, K2) repeat until the last stitch, knit it (K1).

Row 6: Purl all the stitches.

Row 7: K1, (K2, K2tog, YO, K3) repeat until the last stitch, knit it (K1).

Row 8: Purl all the stitches.

Row 9: K1, (K1, K2tog, YO, K4) repeat until the last stitch, knit it (K1).

Row 10: Purl all the stitches.

Row 11: K1, (K5, YO, SKP) until the last stitch, knit it (K1).

Row 12: Purl all the stitches.

Row 13: K2, (K5, YO, SKP) repeat until the end of the row.

Row 14: Purl all the stitches.

Row 15: K1, (YO, SKP, K5) repeat until the last stitch, knit it (K1).

Row 16: Purl all the stitches.

Row 17: K1, (K1, YO, SKP, K4) repeat until the last stitch, knit it (K1).

Row 18: Purl all the stitches.

Row 19: K1, (K2, YO, SKP, K3) repeat until the last stitch, knit it (K1).

Row 20: Purl all the stitches.

Repeat from the first row until you reach the desired length.

Shells Lace Stitch

Cast on a number of stitches that can be divided by 7 Add 3.

Row 1: SL1, K1, (YO, SKP, K5) repeat parenthesis until the last stitch, knit it (K1).

Row 2: SL1, purl all the stitches.

Row 3: SL1, K1, (YO, K1, SKP, K4) repeat parenthesis until the last stitch, knit it (K1).

Row 4: SL1, purl all the stitches.

Row 5: SL1, K1, (YO, K2, SKP, K3) repeat parenthesis until the last stitch, knit it (K1).

Row 6: SL1, purl all the stitches.

Row 7: SL1, K1, (YO, K3, SKP, K2) repeat parenthesis until the last stitch, knit it (K1).

Row 8: SL1, purl all the stitches.

Row 9: SL1, K1, (YO, K4, SKP, K1) repeat parenthesis until the last stitch, knit it (K1).

Row 10: SL1, purl all the stitches.

Row 11: SL1, K1, (YO, K5, SKP) repeat parenthesis until the last stitch, knit it (K1).

Row 12: SL1, purl all the stitches.

Continue on, repeating from the first row until you reach the desired length.

Fishtail Lace Stitch

Cast on a number of stitches that can be divided by 8+1.

Row 1: K1, (YO, K2, SK2P, K2, YO, K1) "SK2P" means slip stitch, k2tog, pass slip stitch over. Repeat what is in the parenthesis until the end of the row.

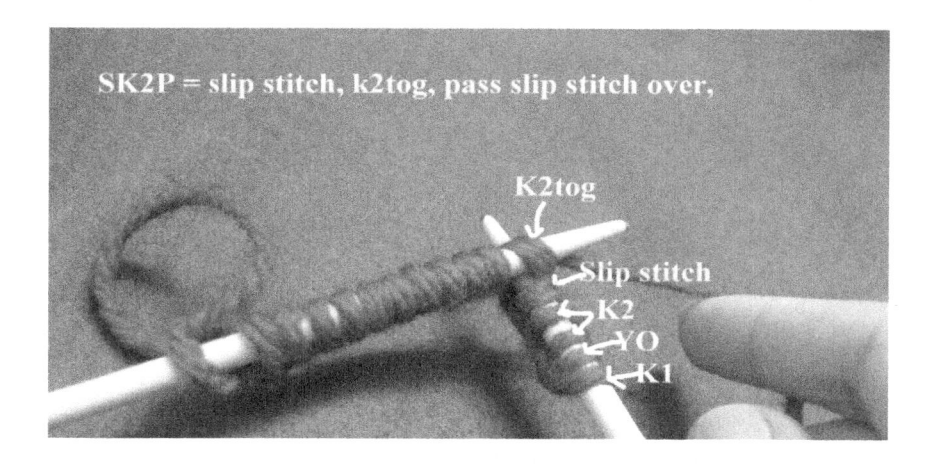

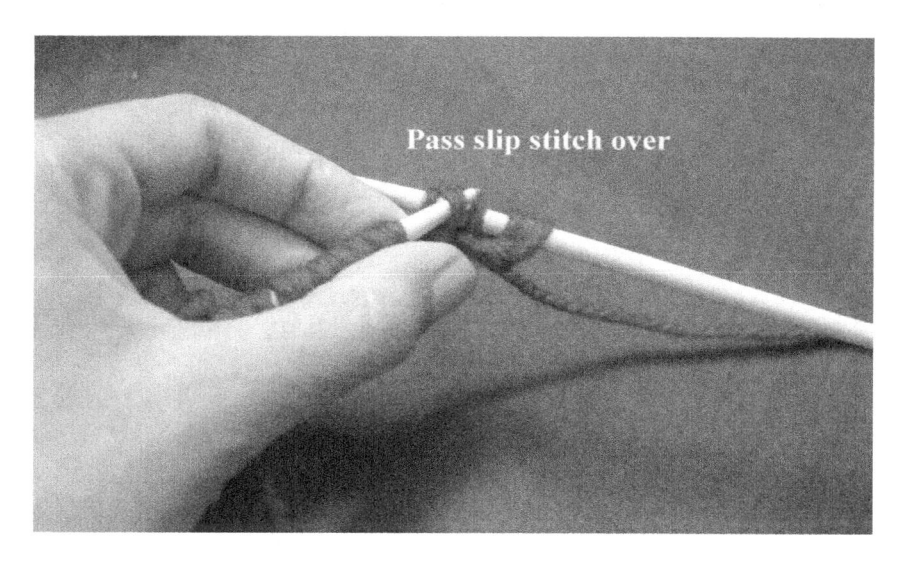

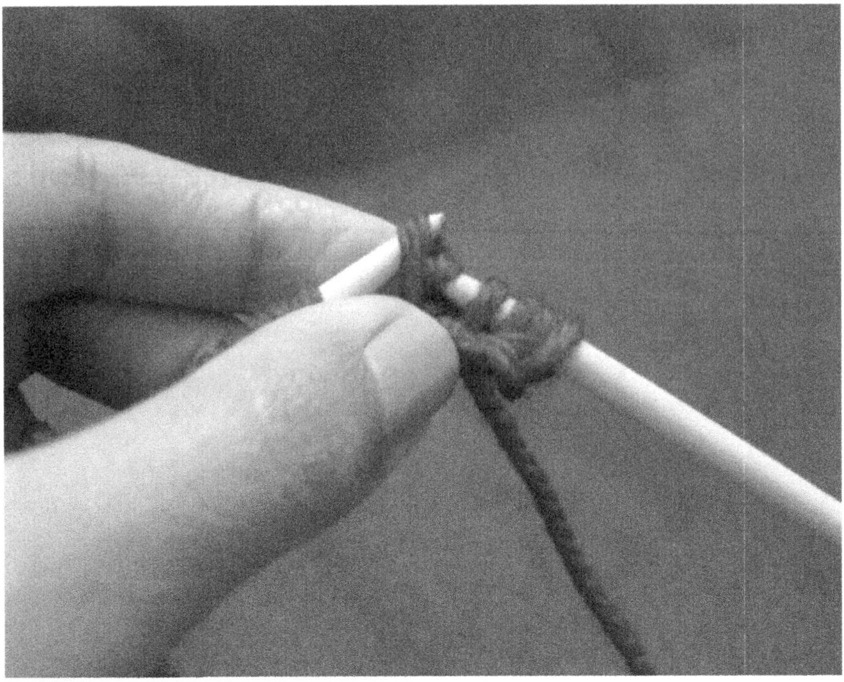

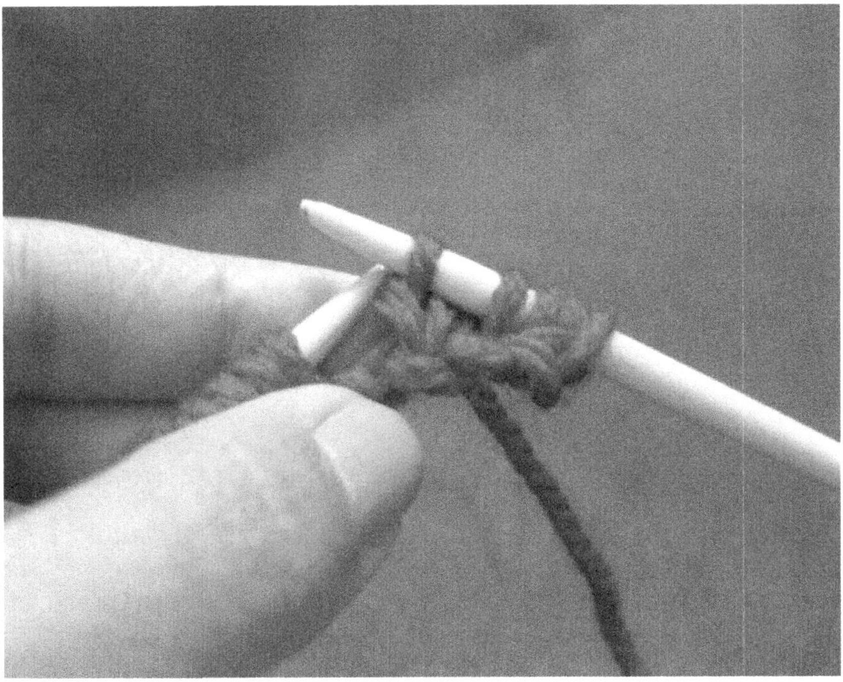

Row 2: Purl all the stitches.

Row 3: K2, (YO, K1, SK2P, K1, YO, K3) repeat parenthesis until the last 7 stitches of the row (YO, K1, SK2P, K1, YO, K2).

Row 4: Purl all the stitches.

Row 5: K3 (YO, SK2P, YO, K5) repeat parenthesis until the last 6 stitches of the row (YO, SK2P, YO, K3).

Row 6: Purl all the stitches. Continue on, repeating from the first row until you reach the desired length.

Butterfly Stitch

Cast on a number of stitches that can be divided by 8+2.

Row 1: Knit all the stitches.

Row 2: Purl all the stitches.

Row 3: K1, (K2, K2tog, YOX2, SKP, K2) repeat the parentheses until the last stitch, knit it (K1).

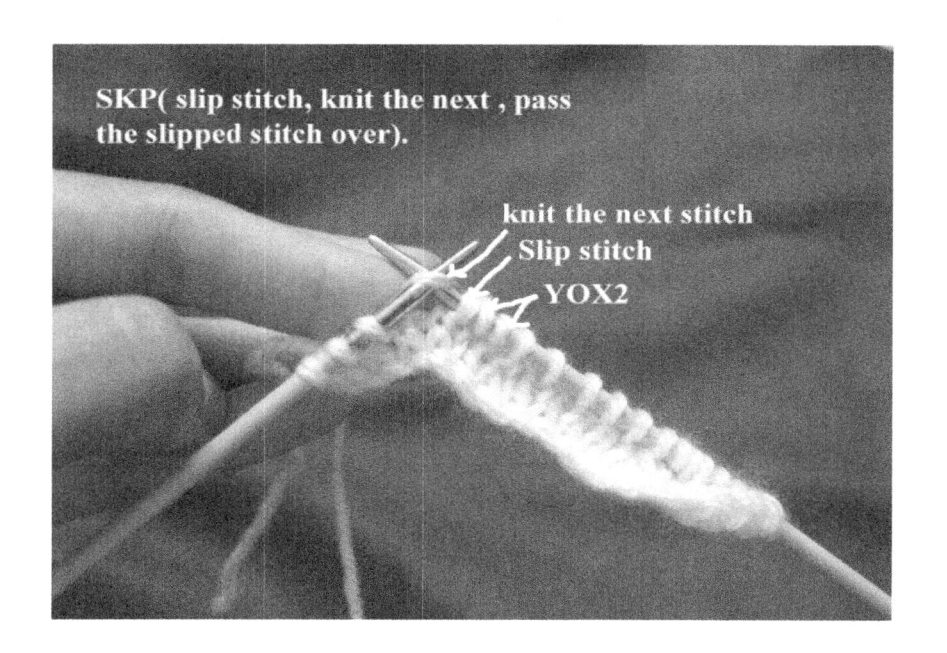

SKP(slip stitch, knit the next , pass the slipped stitch over).

knit the next stitch
Slip stitch
YOX2

pass the slipped stitch over

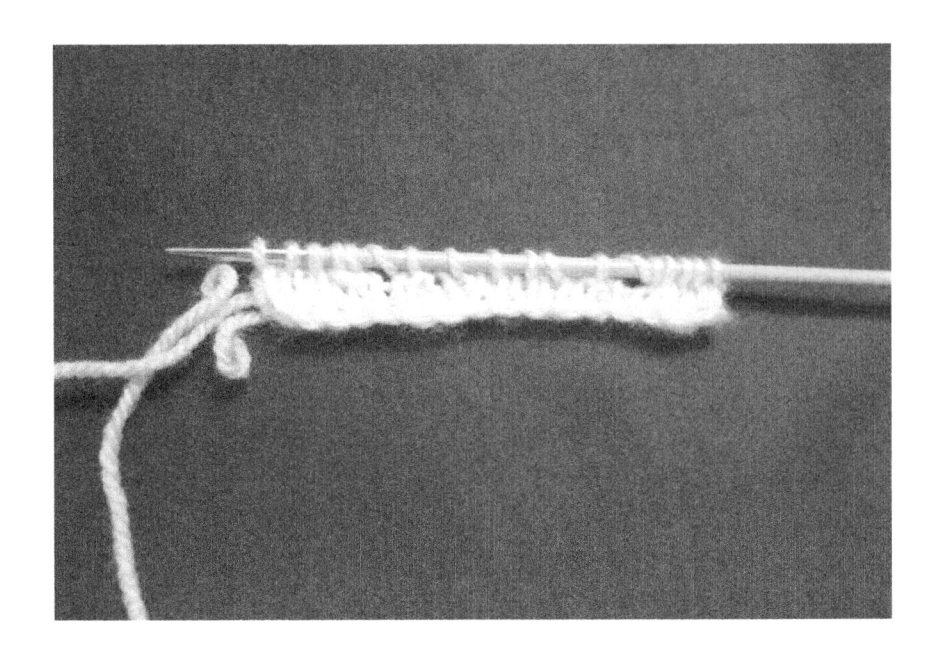

Row 4: Purl all the stitches. When you reach YOX2, slip them and do YOX2 with the yarn in front.

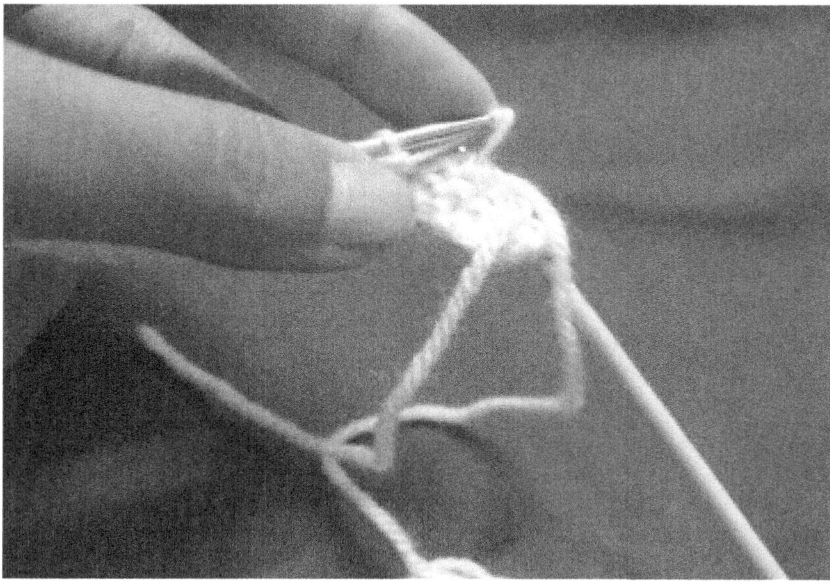

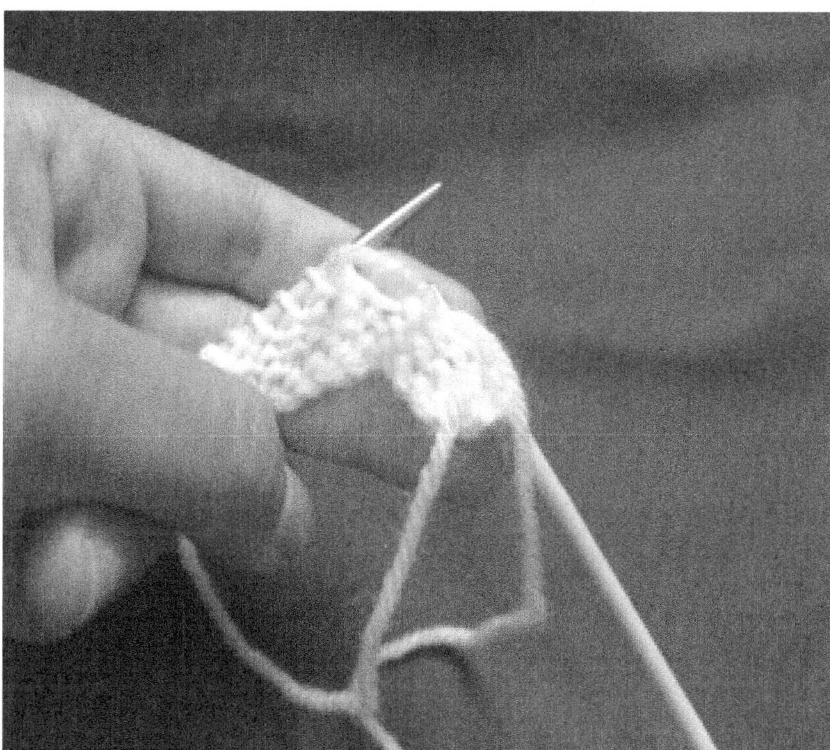

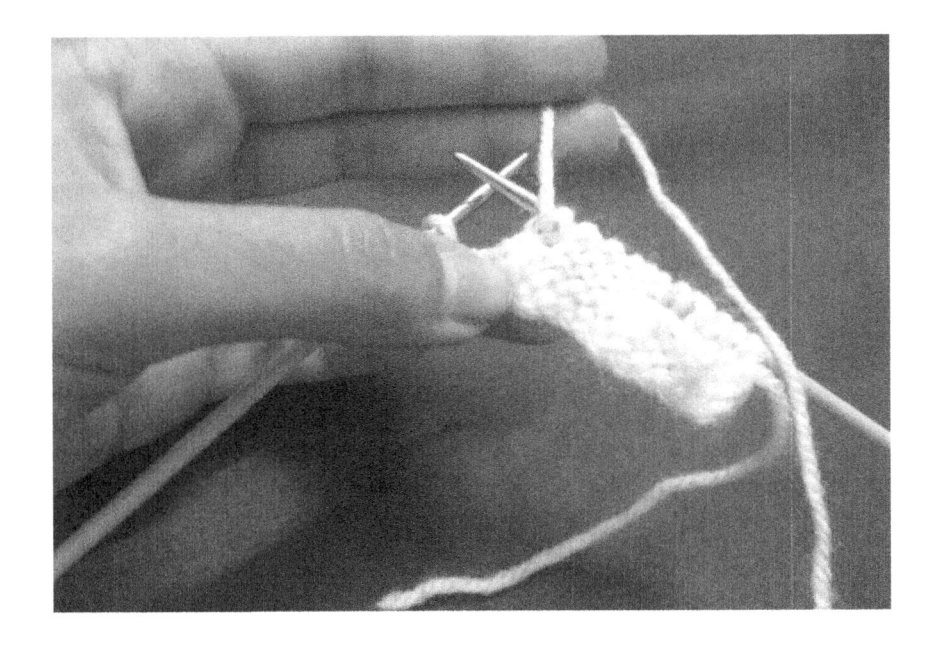

YOX2 with the yarn in front

YOX2 with the yarn in front

Row 5: K1, (K1, K2tog, YOX2, Slip the previous YO2X, SKP, K1) repeat the parenthesis until the last stitch, knit it (K1).

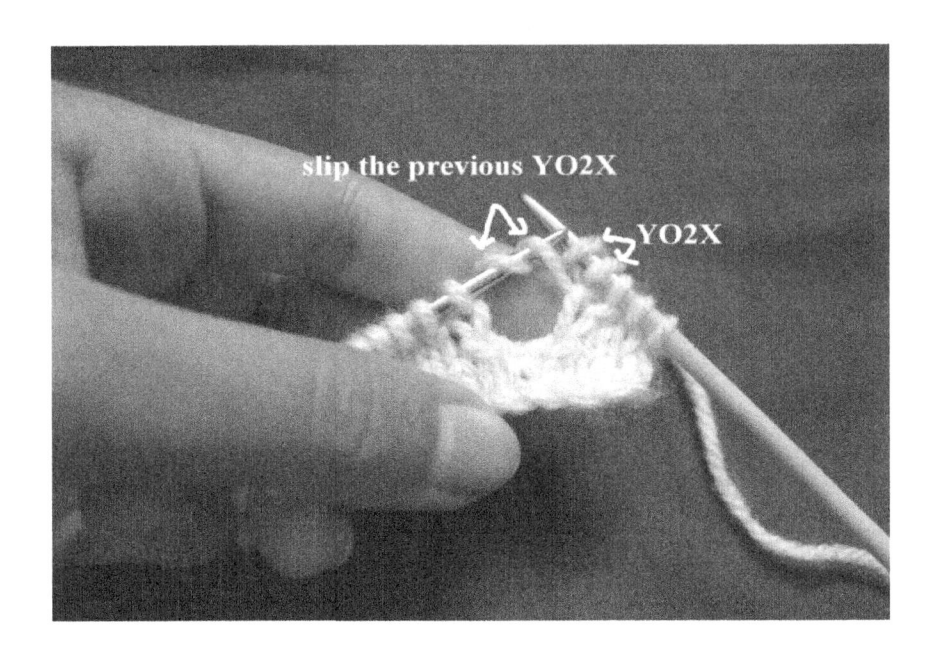

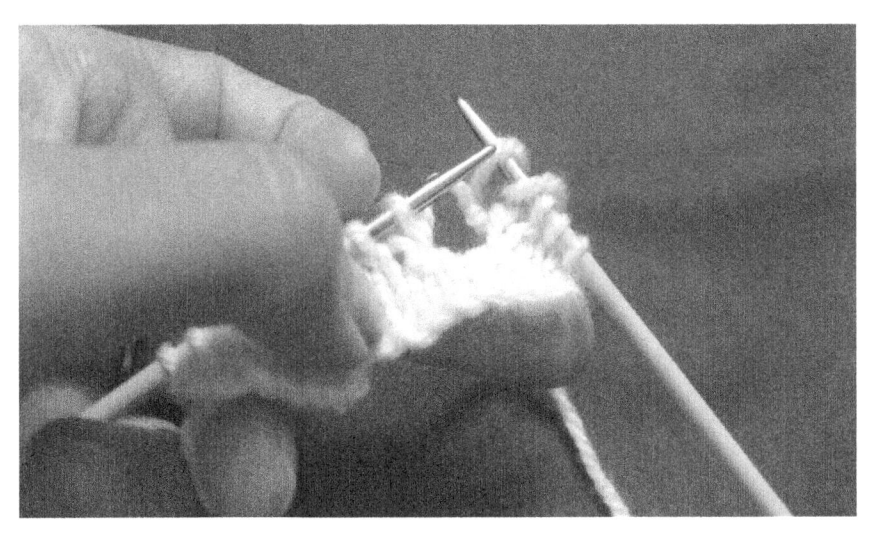

Row 6: Purl all the stitches. When you reach YOX2, slip them. Do YOX2 with the yarn in front.

Row 7: K1, (K2tog, YO2X, Slip the previous YO2X, SKP) repeat the parenthesis until the last stitch, knit it (K1).

Row 8: Purl all the stitches. When you reach the YOX2, slip them. Do YOX2 with the yarn in front.

Row 9: K1,(K1, YO2X, Slip the previous YO2X, put the six slipped stitches from the previous row on the left needle and knit them as one K stitch, YO2X, K1) repeat the parenthesis until the last stitch, knit it (K1).

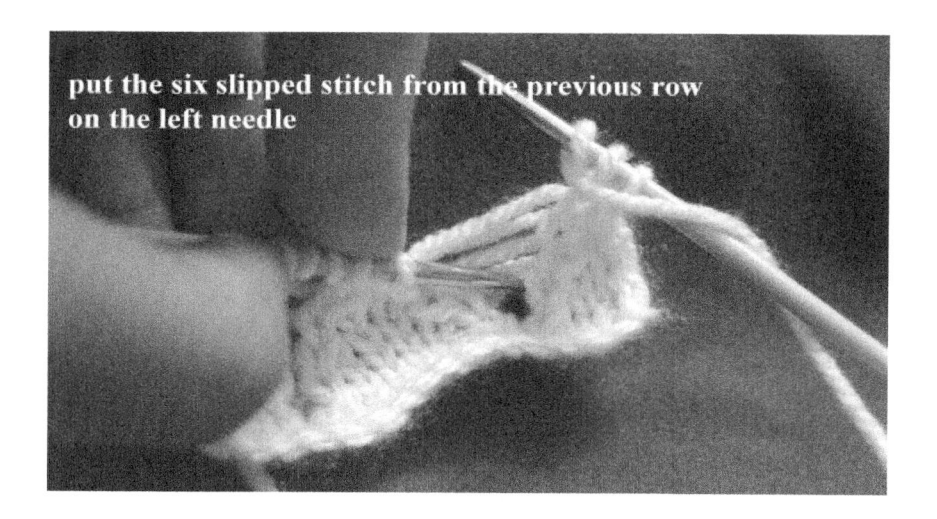

YO2X

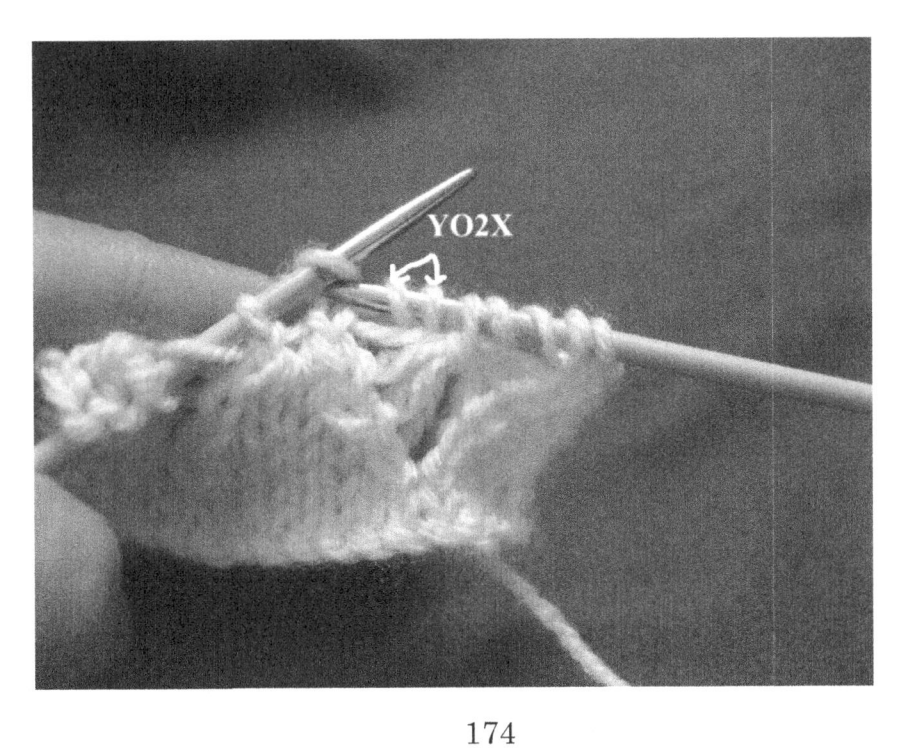

Row 10: K1, (P1, on the YO do PKP, P1, pass the previous stitch over the purl stitch, on the YO, PKP, P1). "PKP" means purl, knit, and purl on the same stitch. Repeat the parenthesis until the last stitch, knit it (K1).

Don't slip the YO2X yet

Put the yarn in the back in knit in the same YO2X and don't slip the YO2X yet bring the yarn to the front and purl into the same YO2X

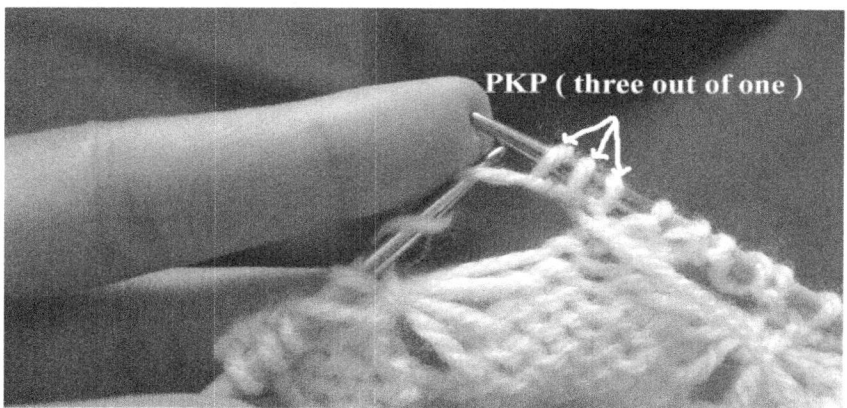

PKP (three out of one)

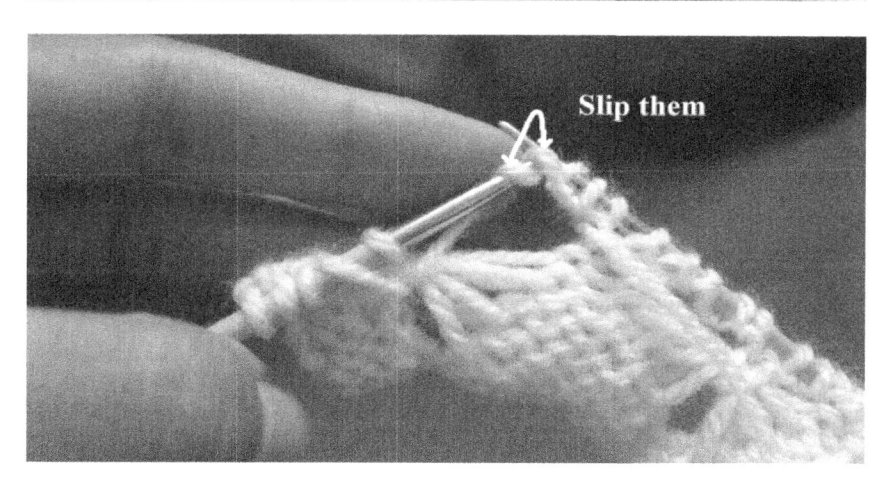

Slip them

pass the previous stitch over the purl stitch

PKP

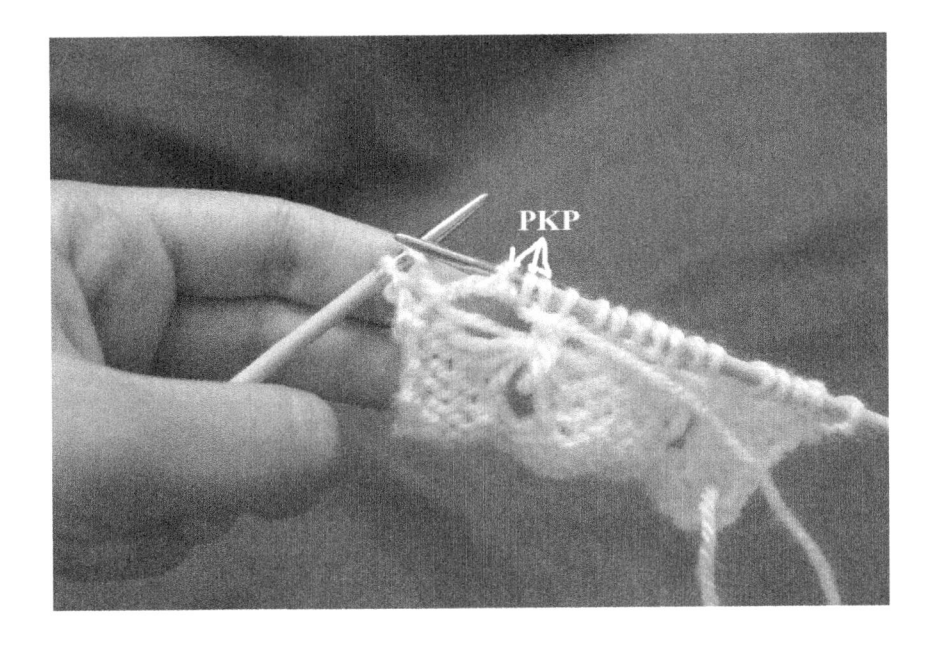

Repeat from the first row until you reach the desired length.

Leaves Stitch

Cast on a number of stitches that can be divided by 29+2.

Row 1: K1, (K1, SK2P, K9, YO, K1, YO, P2, YO, K1, YO, K9, SK2P) repeat parenthesis until the last stitch, knit it (K1).

Row 2: P1, (P13, K2, P14) repeat parenthesis until the last stitch, knit it (K1).

Row 3: K1, (K1, SK2P, K8, YO, K1, YO, K1, P2, K1, YO, K1, YO, K8, SK2P) repeat parenthesis until the last stitch, knit it (K1).

Row 4: P1, (P13, K2, P14) repeat parenthesis until the last stitch, knit it (K1).

Row 5: K1, (K1, SK2P, K7, YO, K1, YO, K2, P2, K2, YO, K1, YO, K7, SK2P) repeat parenthesis until the last stitch, knit it (K1).

Row 6: P1, (P13, K2, P14) repeat parenthesis until the last stitch, knit it (K1).

Row 7: K1, (K1, SK2P, K6, YO, K1, YO, K3, P2, K3, YO, K1, YO, K6, SK2P) repeat parenthesis until the last stitch, knit it (K1).

Row 8: P1, (P13, K2, P14) repeat parenthesis until the last stitch, knit it (K1).

Row 9: K1, (K1, SK2P, K5, YO, K1, YO, K4, P2, K4, P2, K4, YO, K1, YO, K5, SK2P) repeat parenthesis until the last stitch, knit it (K1).

Row 10: P1, (P13, K2, P14) repeat parenthesis until the last stitch, knit it (K1).

Repeat the ten rows from the first row until you reach the desired length.

Bucket Stitch

Cast on a number of stitches that can be divided by 10+2.

Row 1: (P2, K8) repeat parenthesis until the last 2 stitches, purl them (P2).

Row 2: Purl all the stitches.

Row 3: (P2, K8) repeat parenthesis until the last 2 stitches, purl them (P2).

Row 4: K2, (P8, K2) repeat parenthesis until the end of the row.

Row 5: (P2, K8) repeat to the last 2 stitches, purl them (P2).

Row 6: K2, (P8, K2) repeat parenthesis until the end of the row.

Row 7: (P2, K2tog, K4, K2tog) repeat to the last 2 stitches, purl them (P2).

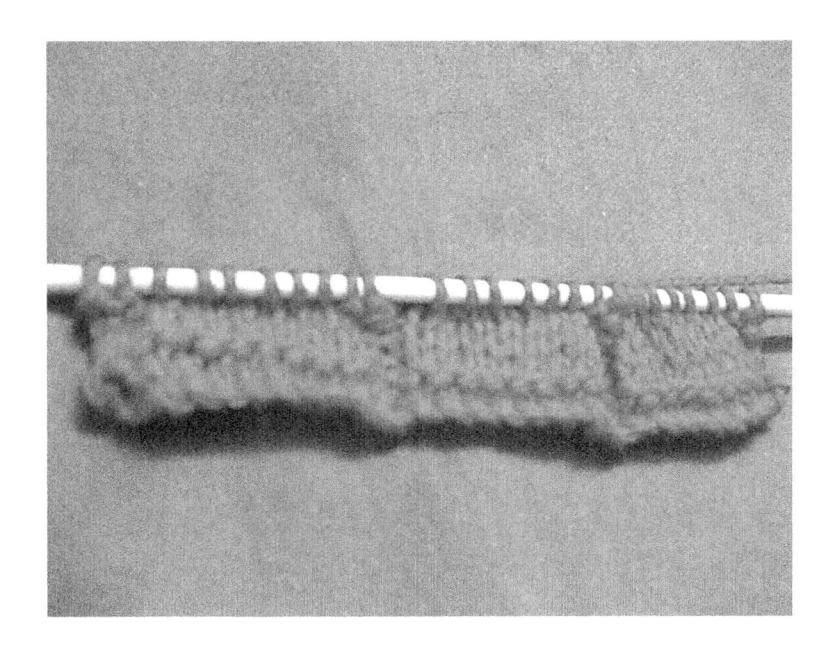

Row 8: K2, (P6, K2) repeat parenthesis until the end of the row.

Row 9: (P2, K2tog, K2, K2tog) repeat to the last 2 stitches, purl them (P2).

Row 10: K2, (P4, K2) repeat parenthesis until the end of the row.

Row 11: (P2, K2tog, K2tog) repeat to the last 2 stitches, purl them (P2).

Row 12: K2, (P2tog, K2tog) repeat parenthesis until the end of the row.

Row 13: (P2, cast on 8 stitches with your finger) repeat until the last 2 stitches, purl them (P2).

Insert the needle into the loop

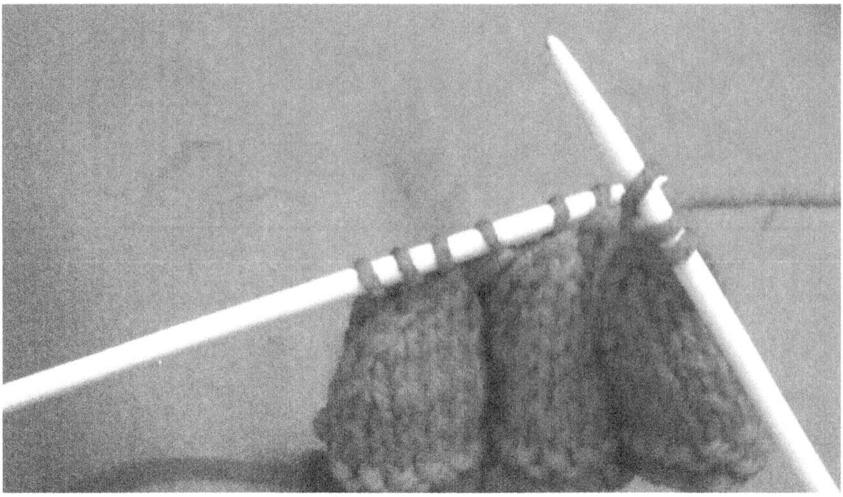

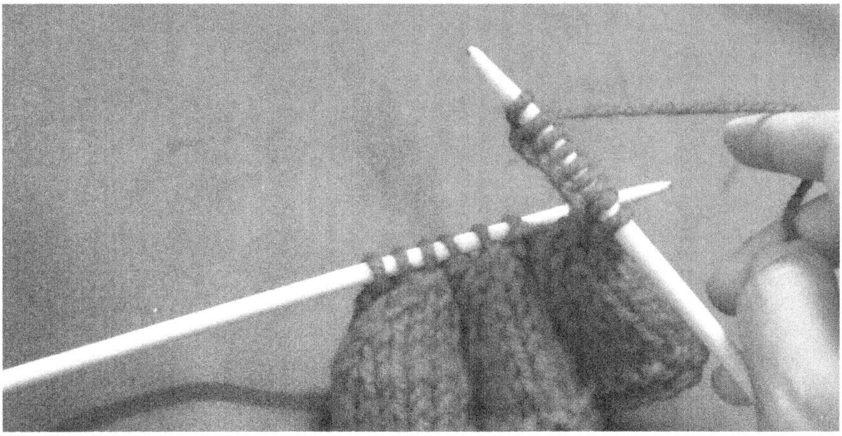

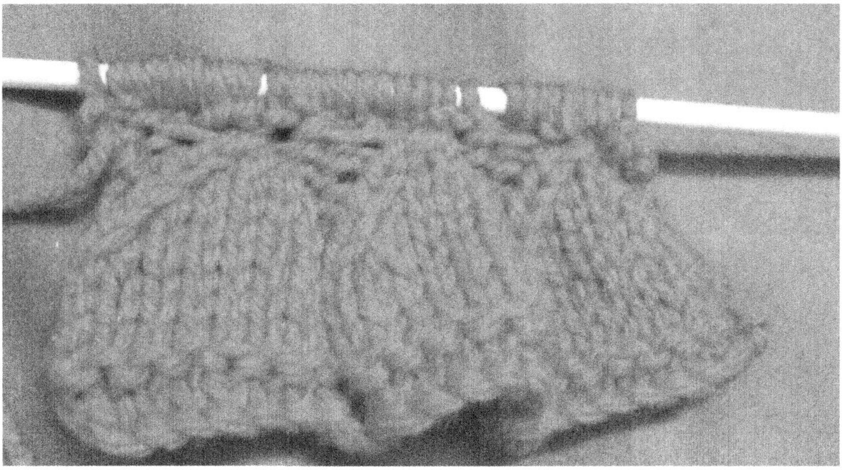

Repeat the thirteen rows from the second row until you reach the desired length.

Lace Heart Stitch

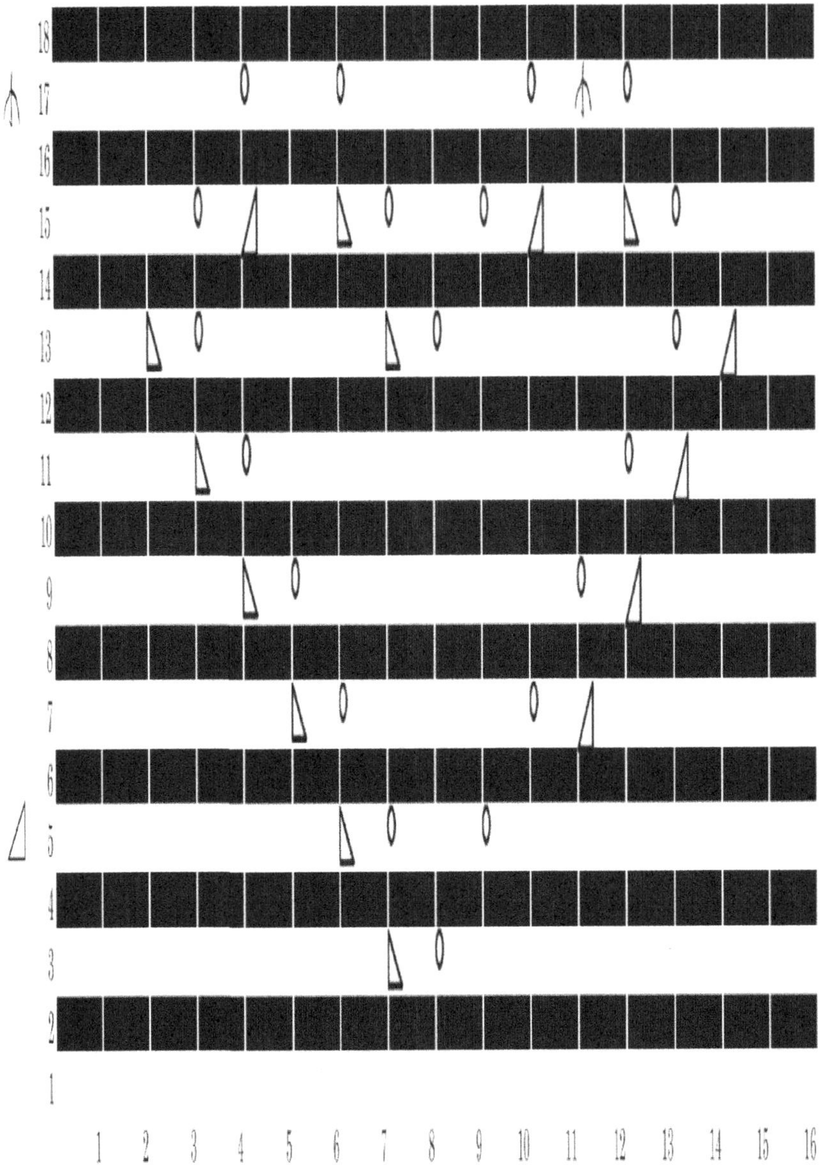
18
17
16
15
14
13
12
11
10
9
8
7
6
5
4
3
2
1
1 2 3 4 5 6 7 8 9 10 11 12 13 14 15 16

The key to the pattern:

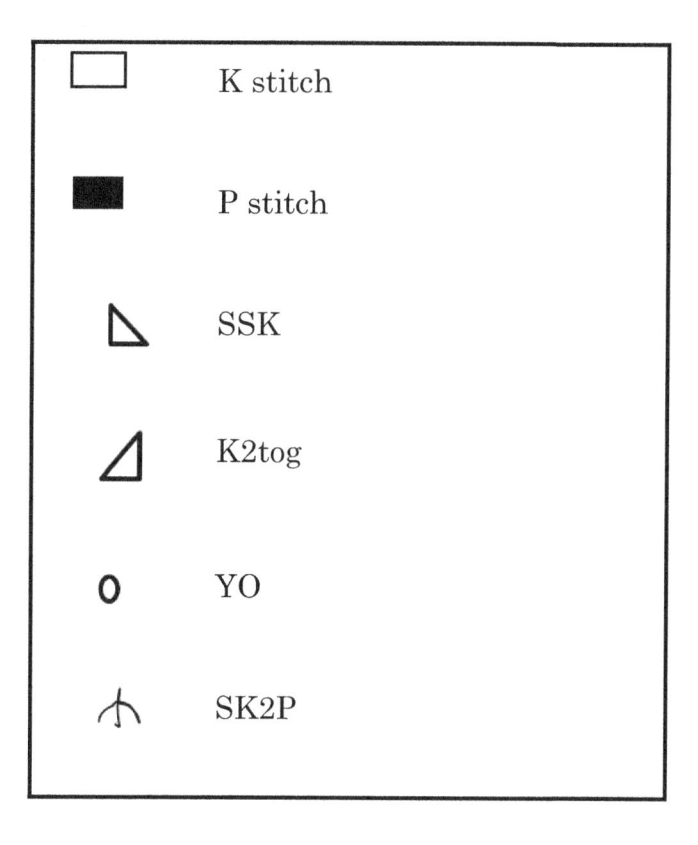

☐	K stitch
■	P stitch
◹	SSK
◸	K2tog
O	YO
⋏	SK2P

Cast on a number of stitches that can be divided by 14+2.

In flat knitting, read the chart from the left side in even rows and from the right in the odd rows.

In round knitting, read every row from right to left.

Row 1: Knit all the stitches.

Row 2: Purl all the stitches.

Row 3: K1, (K6, YO, SSK, K6) repeat parenthesis until the last stitch, knit it (K1).

Row 4: Purl all the stitches.

Row 5: K1, (K4, K2tog, YO, K1, YO, SSK, K5) repeat parenthesis until the last stitch, knit it (K1).

Row 6: Purl all the stitches.

Row 7: K1, (K3, K2tog, YO, K3, YO, SSK, K4) repeat parenthesis until the last stitch, knit it (K1).

Row 8: Purl all the stitches.

Row 9: K1, (K2, K2tog, YO, K5, YO, SSK, K3) repeat parenthesis until the last stitch, knit it (K1).

Row 10: Purl all the stitches.

Row 11: K1, (K1, K2tog, YO, K7, YO, SSK, K2) repeat parenthesis until the last stitch, knit it (K1).

Row 12: Purl all the stitches.

Row 13: K1, (K2tog, YO, K4, YO, SSK, K3, YO, SSK, K1) repeat parenthesis until the last stitch, knit it (K1).

Row 14: Purl all the stitches.

Row 15: K1, (K1, YO, SSK, K1, K2tog, YO, K1, YO, SSK, K1, K2tog YO, K2) repeat parenthesis until the last stitch, knit it (K1).

Row 16: Purl all the stitches.

Row 17: K1, (K2, YO, SK2P, YO, K3, YO, SK2P, YO, K3) repeat parenthesis until the last stitch, knit it (K1).

Row 18: Purl all the stitches.

Repeat the eighteen rows from the first row until you reach the desired length.

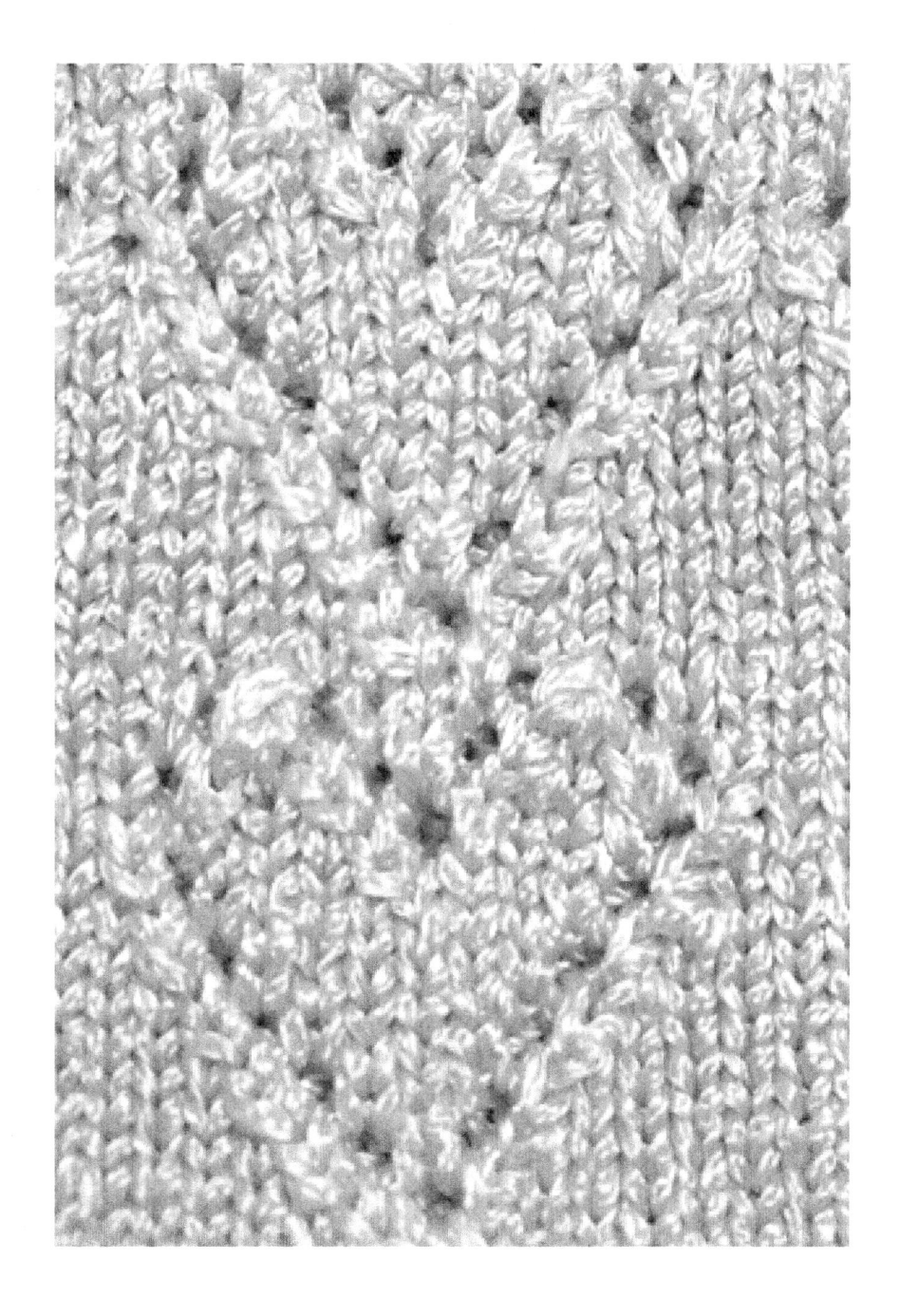

Next, we will learn how to knit the Old Shale pattern stitch.

Old Shale

Cast on a number of stitches that can be divided by 18.

Row 1: Knit all the stitches.

Row 2: Purl all the stitches.

Row 3: (K2tog, K2tog, K2tog, YO, K1, YO, K1, YO, K1 YO, K1, YO, K1, YO, K1, K2tog, K2tog, K2tog) repeat what parenthesis until the end of the row.

Row 4: Knit all the stitches.

Repeat the four rows from the first row until you reach the desired length.

Stockinette Chevron

Cast on a number of stitches that can be divided by 18.

Row 1: Knit all the stitches.

Row 2: Purl all the stitches.

Row 3: (K2tog, K2tog, K2tog, KFB, KFB, KFB, KFB, KFB, KFB, K2tog, K2tog, K2tog) repeat parenthesis until the end of the row.

Row 4: Purl all the stitches.

Repeat the four rows from the first row until you reach the desired length.

Lace Stitch

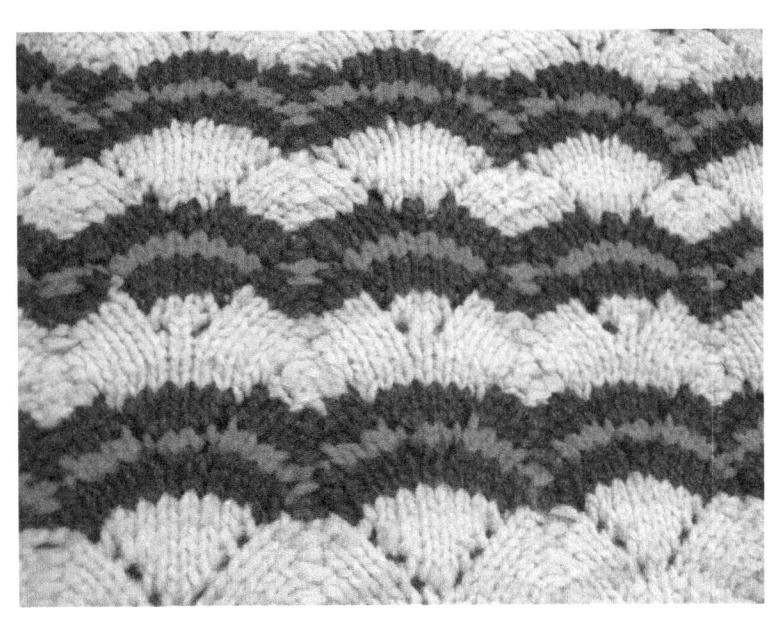

You can do this stitch with one color or alternate with a lot of colors.

Cast on a number of stitches that can be divided by 12+1

Row 1: P2tog (K4, YO, K1, YO, K4, P3tog) repeat parenthesis until the last 2 stitches. Purl them together P2tog.

Row 2: Purl all the stitches.

Row 3: P2tog (K3, YO, K3, YO, K3, P3tog) repeat parenthesis until the last 2 stitches. Purl them together P2tog.

Row 4: Purl all the stitches.

Row 5: P2tog (K2, YO, K5, YO, K2, P3tog) repeat parenthesis until the last 2 stitches. Purl them together P2tog.

Row 6: Purl all the stitches.

Row 7: P2 tog (K1, YO, K7, YO, K1, P3tog) repeat parenthesis until the last 2 stitches. Purl them together P2tog.

Row 8: Purl all the stitches.

Row 9: P2tog (YO, K9, YO, P3tog) repeat parenthesis until the last 2 stitches. Purl them together P2tog.

Row 10: Purl all the stitches. Repeat the ten rows from the first row until you reach the desired length.

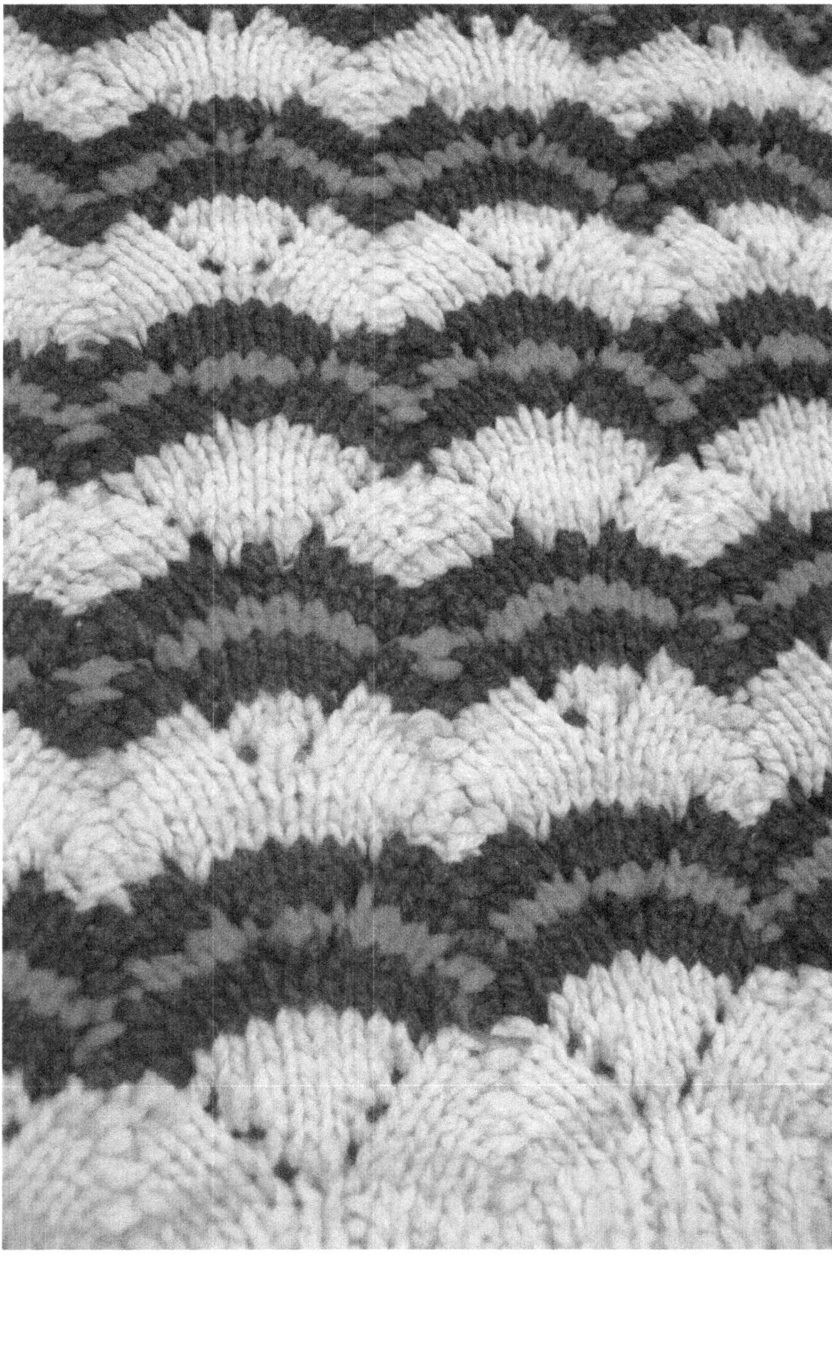

Finishing the Ends

Bind off the stitches until you have only one stitch left.

Cut the yarn. Slip the stitch off the needle. Pass the yarn through it.

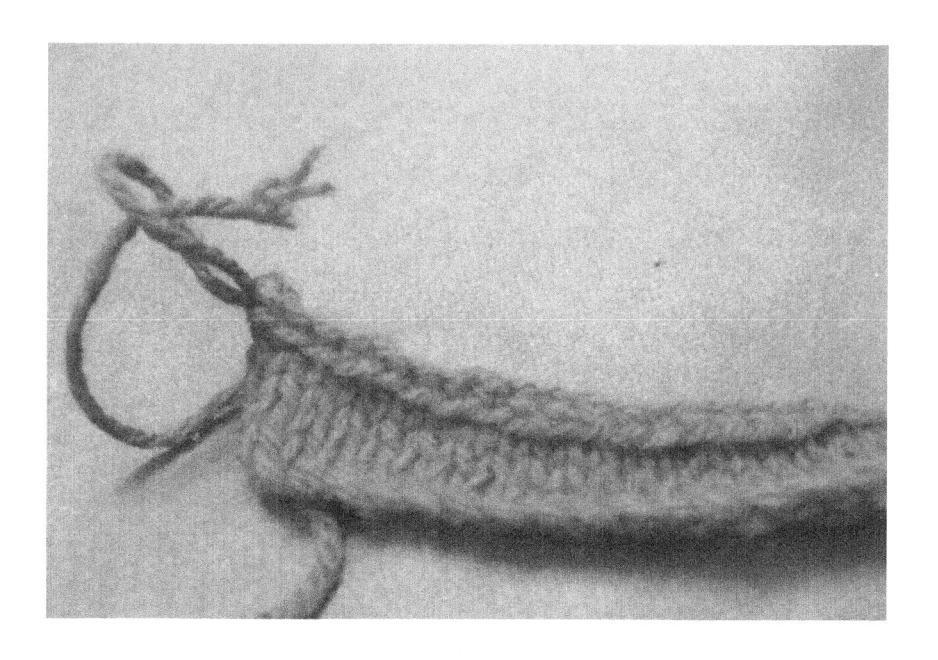

Tighten the knot.

Hide the tail in the back by using a crochet hook.

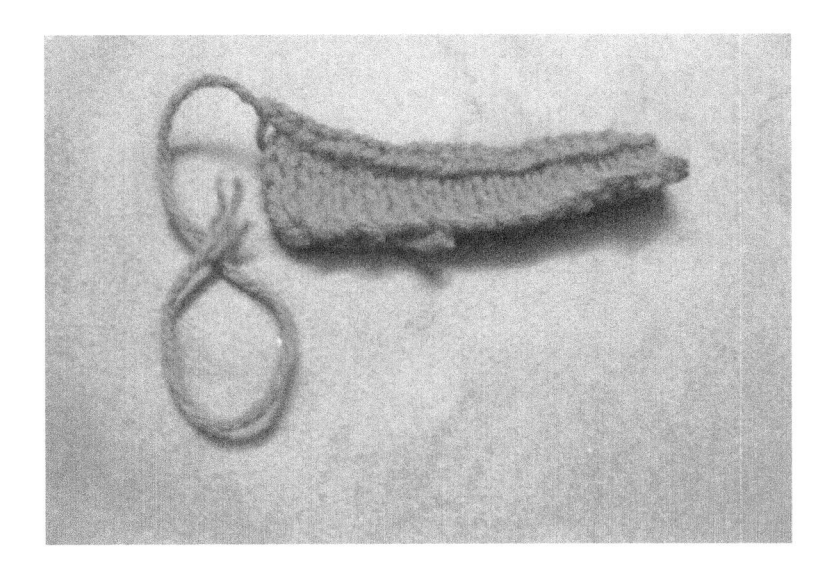

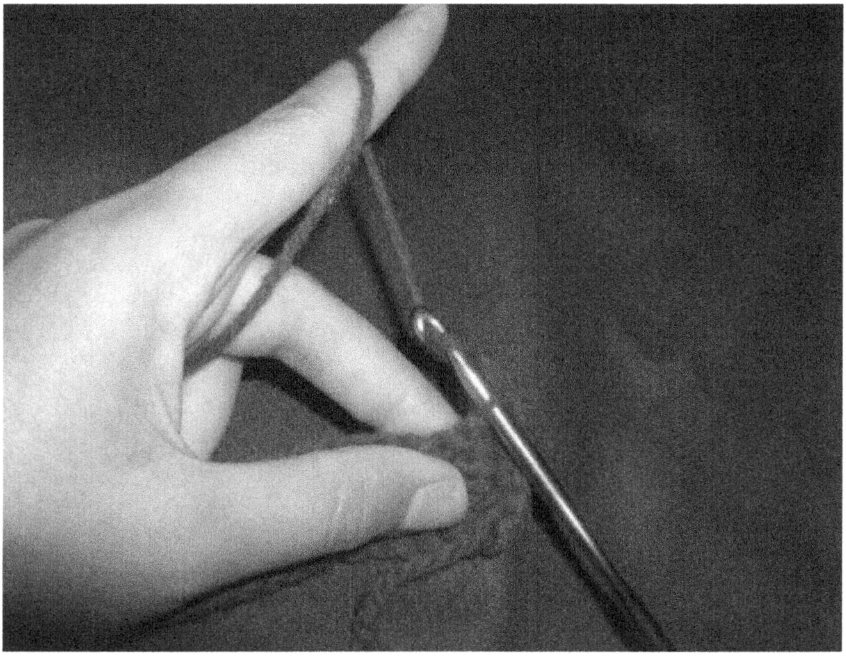

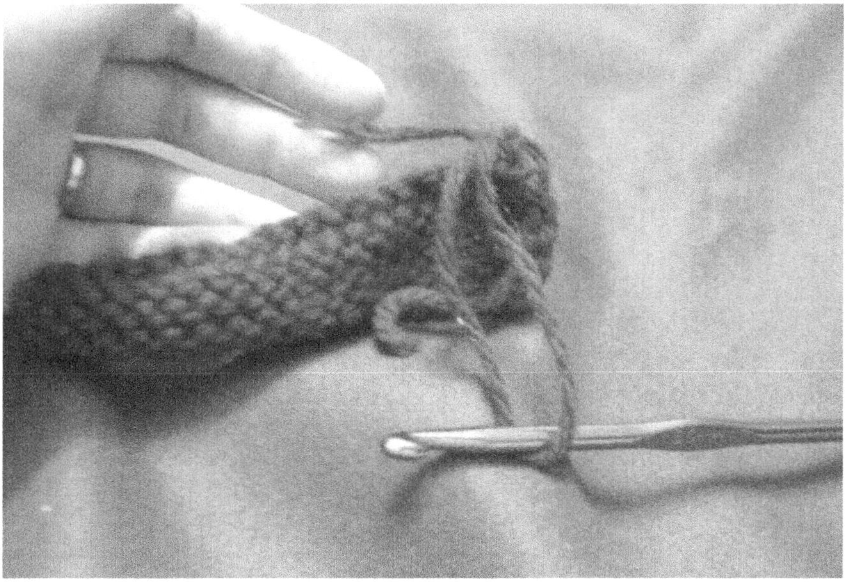

Knitting a Hat

This project simple and classic. You can embellish it and create your own design.

Knitted hats make a great gift!

We are going to use the stockinette and dual rib stitch (2x2).

I used a few types of yarn: Himalaya alpine, 100% dralon acrylic 224 yards, 100 g.

You will need to use:

- Circular needle size 5, 16 inches in circumference
- Stitch marker
- Sewing needle

This pattern is one basic pattern that you can make in five different sizes: baby, toddler, kid, women, and men.

The first number before the parenthesis indicates the baby size, the other numbers inside the parenthesis indicate other pattern sizes.

For example, "42 (48, 54, 60, 66)" means that the baby size is 42, toddler is 48, kid size is 54, women size is 60, and men size is 66.

I have also mentioned a few ideas about how to decorate your finished hat.

Make the Cuff

Step 1: Cast 42 (48, 54, 60, 66) stitches onto the circular needle.

Step 2: Place a marker. Join on for working in the round. Be careful not to twist the stitches.

Round 1: (K2, P2) repeat to the end of the round.

Repeat round 1 four (4, 5, 5, 6) more times.

Knit all rounds until you reach to 5 (5 1/2, 6, 6 1/2, 7) inches from the cast on edge.

Make the Crown

For the baby size hat, start decreasing in round 9.

For the toddler size, start decreasing in round 7.

For the kid size, start decreasing in round 5.

For the women size, start decreasing in round 3.

For the men size, start decreasing in round 1.

Round 1: (K8, K2tog) repeat to the end of the round 60 stitches.

Round 2: Knit all the stitches.

Round 3: (K7, K2tog) repeat to the end of the round 54 stitches.

Round 4: Knit all the stitches.

Round 5: (K6, K2tog) repeat to the end of the round 48 stitches.

Round 6: Knit all the stitches.

Round 7: (K5, K2tog) repeat to the end of the round 42 stitches.

Round 8: Knit all the stitches.

Round 9: (K4, K2tog) repeat to the end of the round 36 stitches.

Round 10: (K3, K2tog) repeat to the end of the round 30 stitches

Round 11: (K2, K2tog) repeat to the end of the round 24 stitches.

Round 12: (K1, K2tog) repeat to the end of the round 18 stitches

Round 13: (K2tog) repeat to the end of the round 12 stitches.

Leave 12 inches for the tail. Cut the yarn. Thread it through the remaining stitches with the sewing needle. Put the tail in the sewing needle.

Pass it through the 12 stitches of Round 13. Pull the tail tightly.

Hat Pattern Variants and Decorations

Change Colors

With color A, cast on and knit the cuff.

With color B, knit the body and the crown.

Pinstripe Hat Variation

With color A, cast on and knit the cuff.

With color B, knit 3 rounds in the body then alternate with color A. You can use as many different colors as you like.

Pom-Poms

Materials:

- ❖ scissors

- ❖ yarn of your choice

- ❖ pen

- ❖ drawing compass (or circle shapes to trace)

- ❖ craft knife

- ❖ a sheet of cardstock paper or cardboard

Step 1: Measure and cut two circles of about 4 inches in diameter. For fuller pom-poms, make the circles larger.

Cut a smaller circle out of the center of each circle. This circle is about 1-inch diameter.

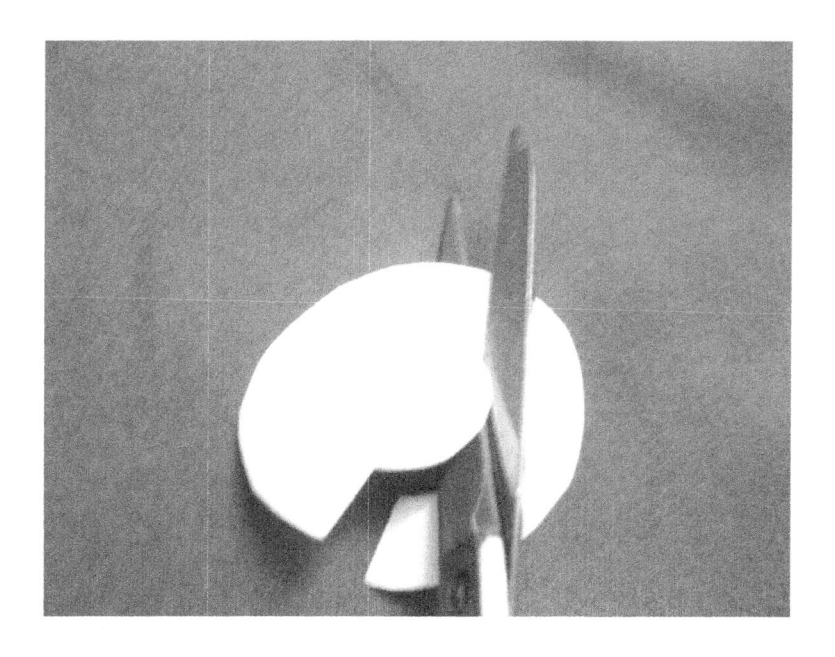

Cut a slit on the side of the circle, making a C shape. Stack the C's on top of each other, leaving the opening.

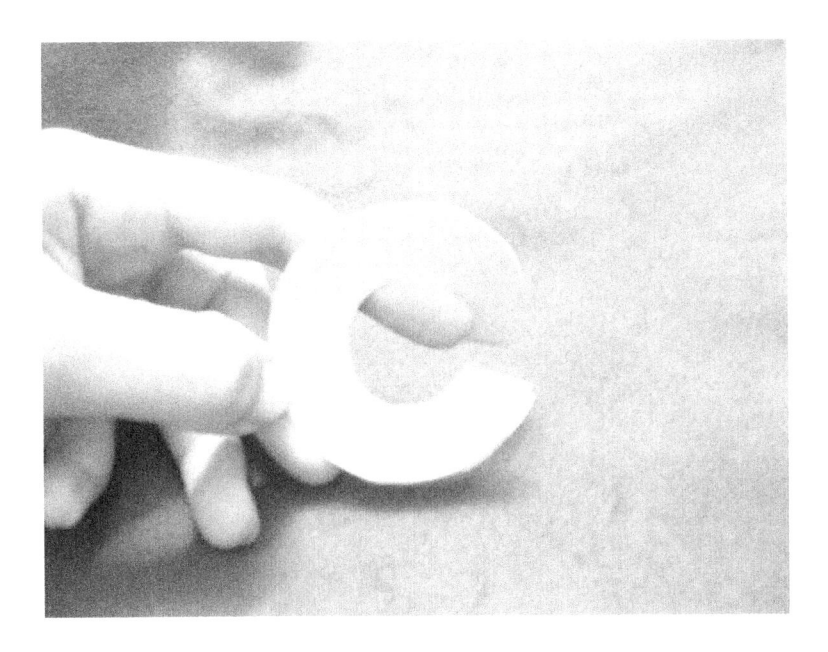

Wrap the yarn on the paper around the C shape.

Wrap a second layer of the yarn on top of the first, changing color if desired.

Use the craft knife and score the yarn around the outside of the C.

put the yarn between the two circles

Put the tail of the yarn between the two circles. Think of it as gathering all of the smaller, cut strings.

Remove the paper. Shape your pom-pom by snipping any longer threads or bulging sections.

Using the sewing needle, affix it onto the hat.

Mary Jane Shoes/Baby Booties

This pattern is super simple. These handmade baby shoes make darling baby shower gifts that any mom-to-be will cherish.

Use the garter stitch.

Materials:

- ❖ cotton yarn 50 g

- ❖ straight knitting needles size 3 mm

- ❖ sewing needle

- ❖ 2 buttons

- ❖ crochet hook

Basic Shoe Pattern

This pattern is for 6 - 10-month size.

The left shoes:

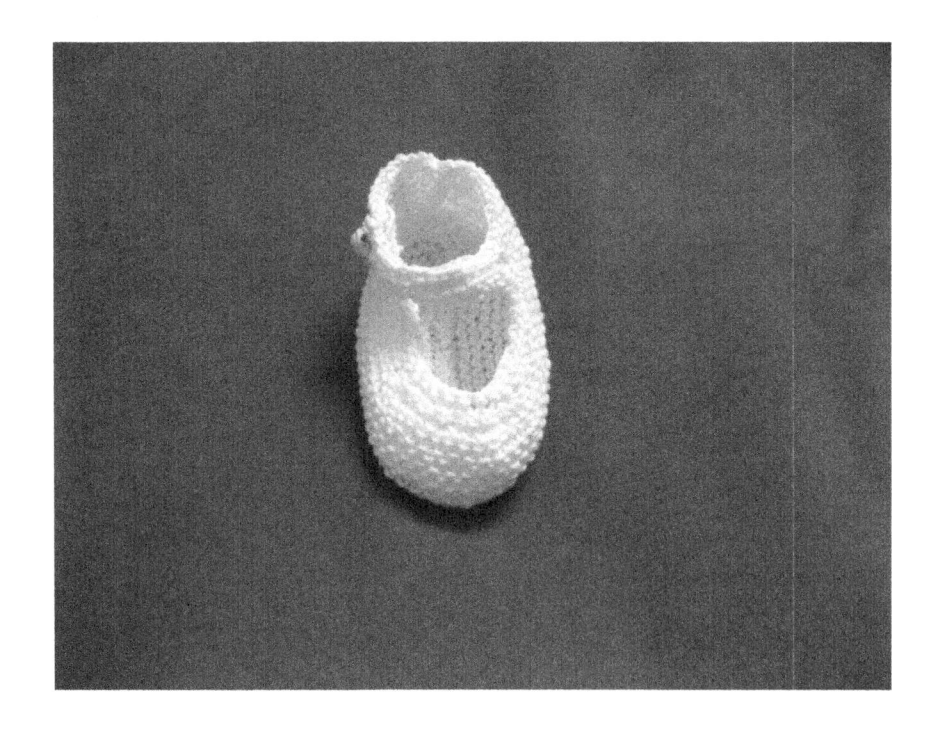

Cast on 43 stitches.

Row 1: Knit all the stitches.

Row 2: Knit all the stitches.

Row 3: Knit all the stitches.

Row 4: (increase row): K1, M1R, K20, M1R, K1, M1R, K20, M1R, K1 (47 stitches).

Row 5: Knit all the stitches.

Row 6: (increase row): K2, M1R, K20, M1R, K3, M1R, K20, M1R, K2 (51 stitches).

Row 7: Knit all the stitches.

Row 8: (increase row): K3, M1R, K20, M1R, K5, M1R, K20, M1R, K3 (55 stitches).

Row 9: Knit all the stitches.

Row 10: (increase row): K4, M1R, K20, M1R, K7, M1R, K20, M1R, K4 (59 stitches).

Rows 11-21: Knit all the stitches.

Row 22: K21, (SSK) four times, K1, (K2tog) four times, K21 (51 stitches).

Row 23: Knit all the stitches.

Row 24: K13, bind off 26 stitches, k13.

Row 25: K13, turn your work and cast on 16 stitches using the cable cast on method (29 stitches total).

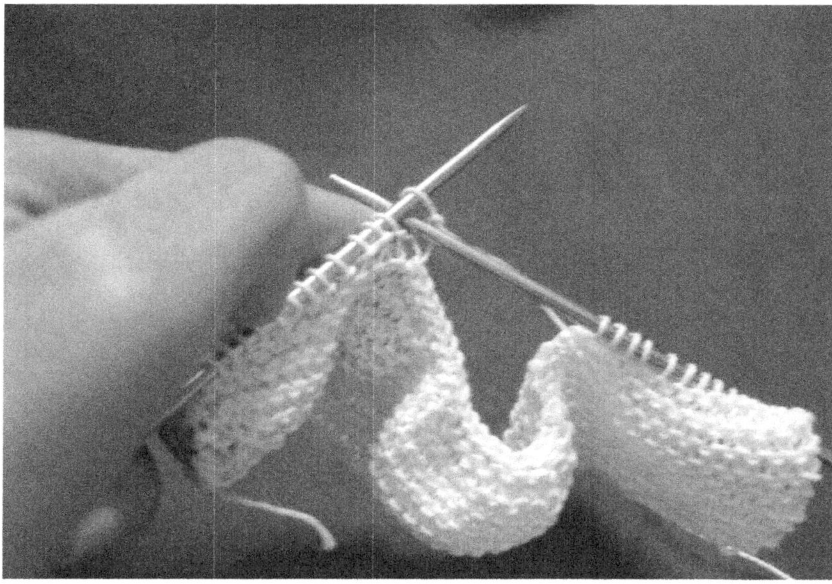

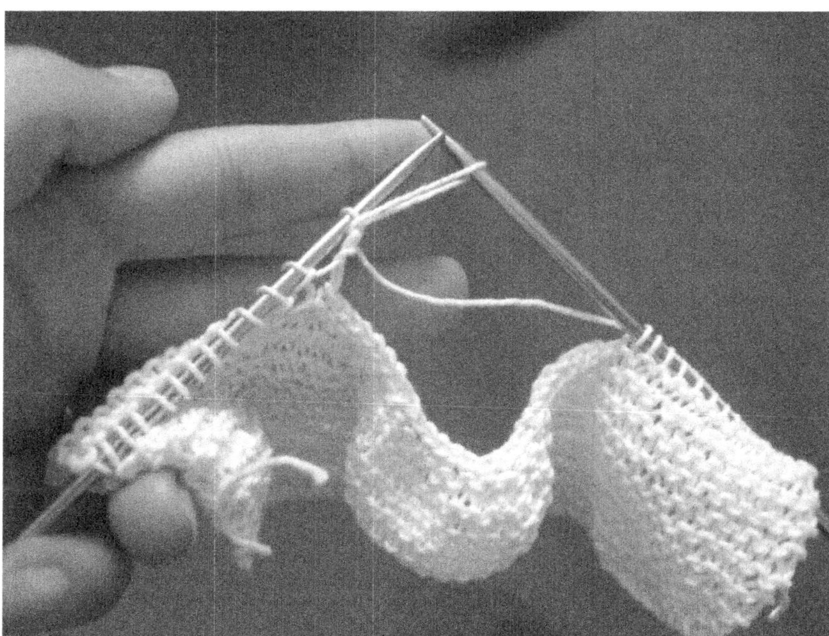

Row 26: Knit all the stitches.

Row 27: K26, K2tog, YO, K1 (buttonhole).

Row 28: Knit all the stitches.

Row 29: Bind off and cut the yarn. Weave the end.

For the 13 stitches on the other needle, rejoin the yarn. Knit through a slip knot.

Knit the next four stitches with both the tail and the working yarn.

Cut the tail and continue knitting with the working yarn.

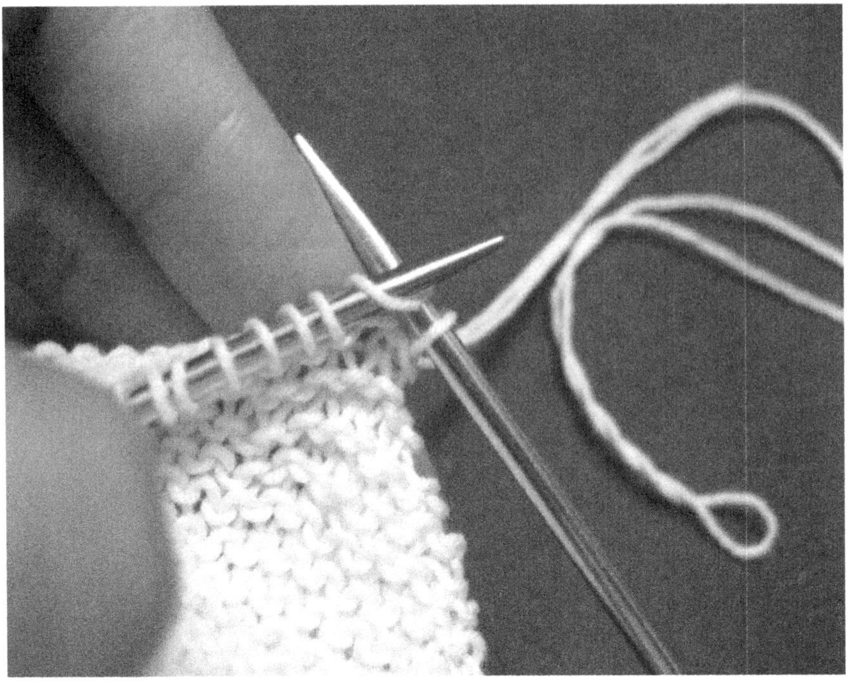

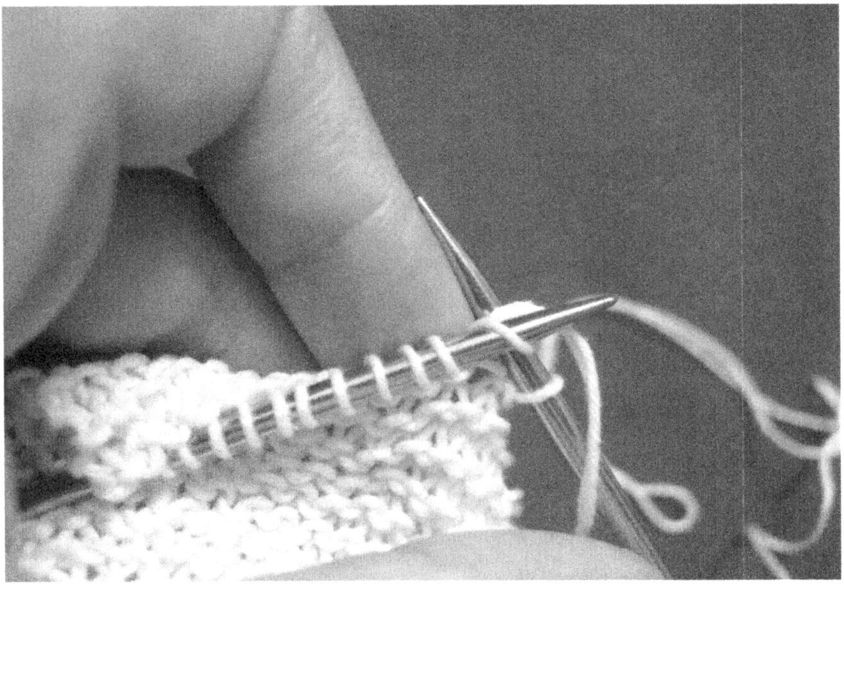

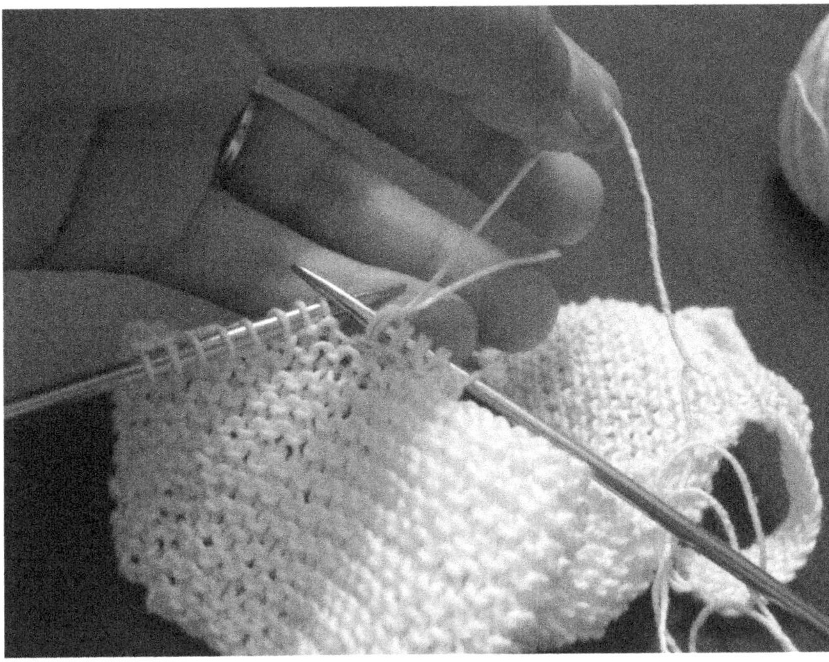

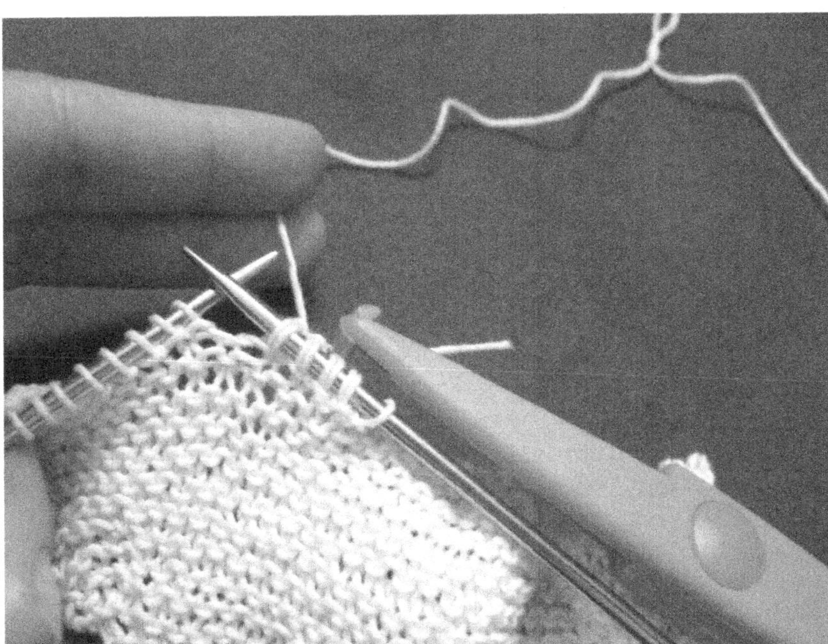

Rows 25-28: Knit all the stitches.

Row 29: Bind off and cut the yarn. Leave a 10-inch tail. This will be for sewing the sides together on the wrong side.

The right shoes:

Work the same as left shoes to **Row 24**.

Rows 25-28: Knit all the stitches.

Row 29: Bind off and cut the yarn. Leave a 10-inch tail for sewing the sides together.

Fold the shoes and sew the wrong sides together. Attach the button.

For the 13 stitches on the other needle, rejoin yarn.

Knit through a slip knot. Cast on 16 stitches by the cable cast- on method (29 stitches total).

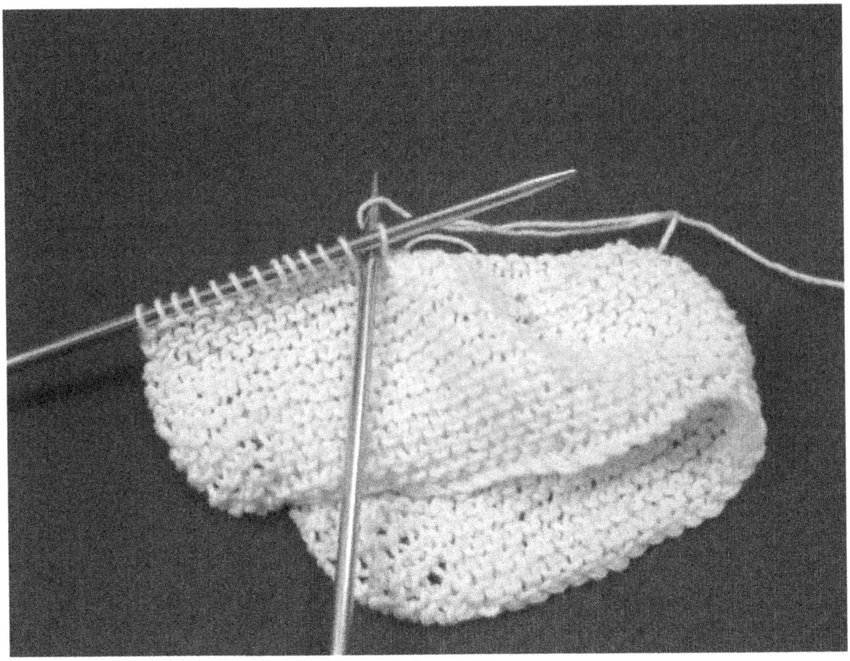

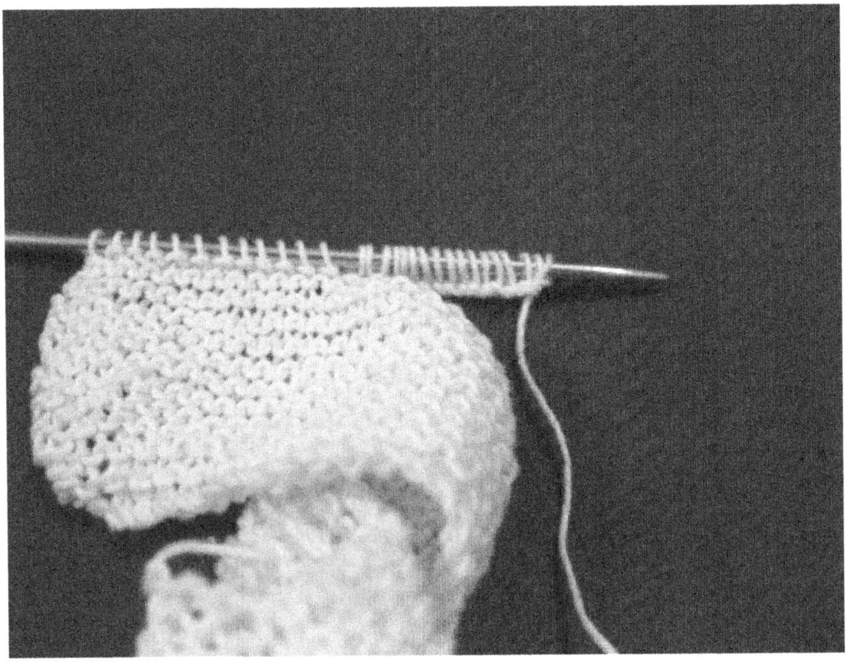

Row 26: Knit all the stitches.

Row 27: K26, K2tog, YO, K1 (buttonhole).

Row 28: Knit all the stitches.

Row 29: Bind off and cut the yarn. Weave the end by using a crochet hook to hide it in the back.

Fold the shoes and sew the wrong sides together. Then attach a button.

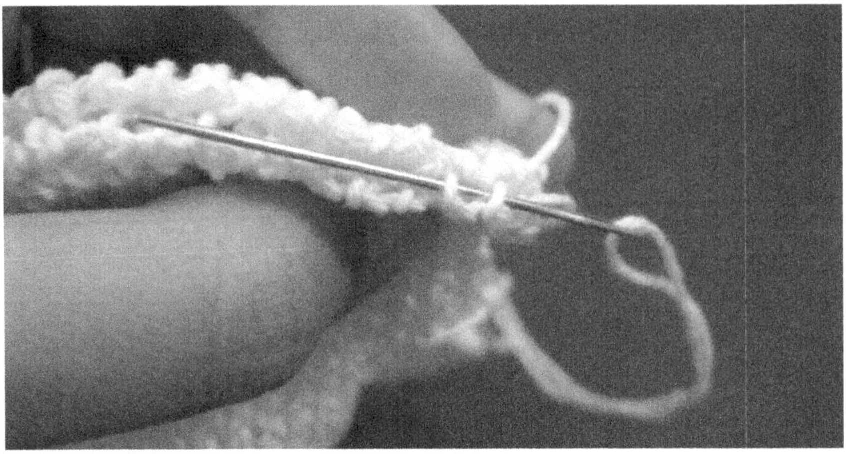

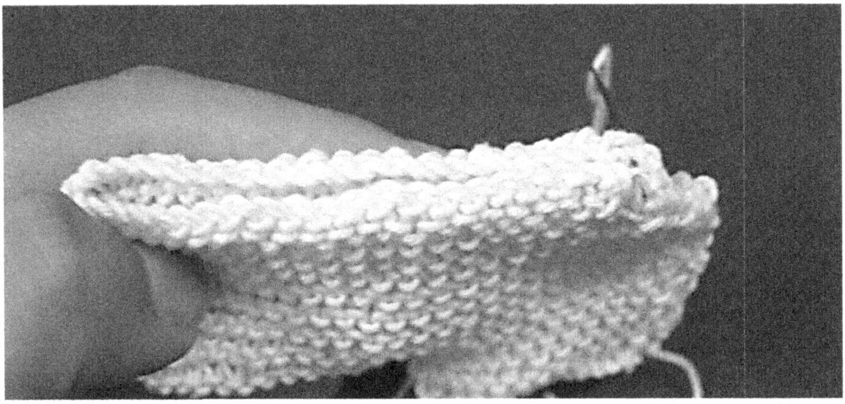

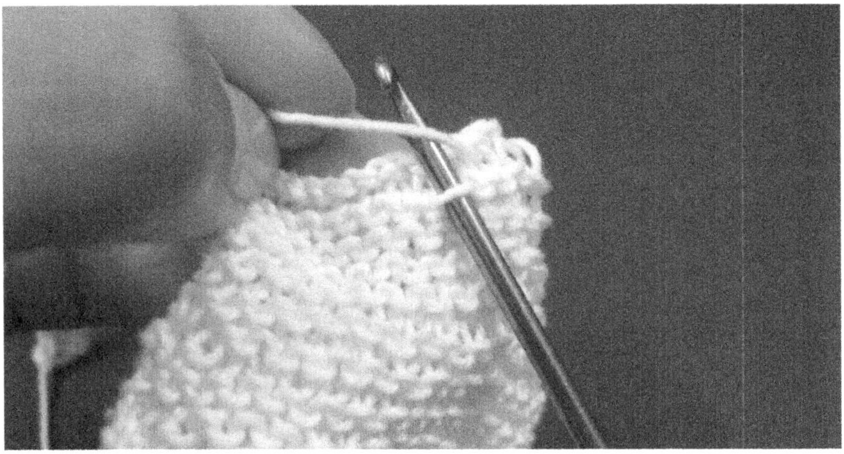

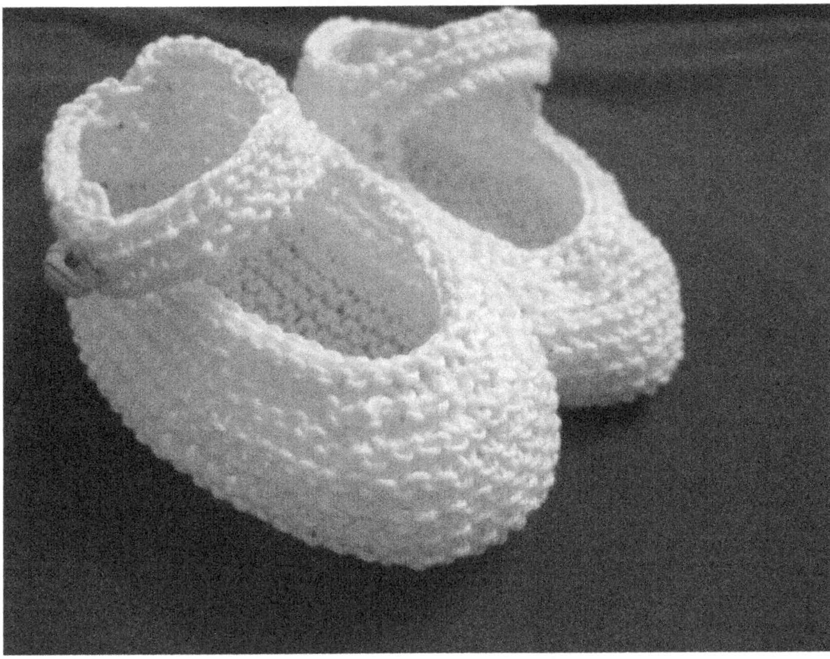

Drop Stitch Scarf

Materials:

- ❖ Alize Burcum 100% acrylic.100 g, 230 yds
- ❖ straight knitting needle size 5 mm

Basic Scarf Pattern

Cast on 23 stitches.

Row 1: Knit all the stitches.

Row 2: Knit all the stitches.

Row 3: Knit all the stitches.

Row 4: Knit all the stitches.

Row 5: Insert your right needle into the first stitch. Wrap the yarn around the two needles.

Put the yarn in between the two needles.

Knit the stitch. Repeat until the end of the row.

Repeat **Rows 1-5** until scarf measures 160 cm (about 63 inches).

Weave in the ends.

Add fringe, if desired.

To add fringe, cut 18 cm (about 7 inches) of the yarn 48 times.

Take three pieces of the fringe at once and tie them to the end by using a crochet hook.

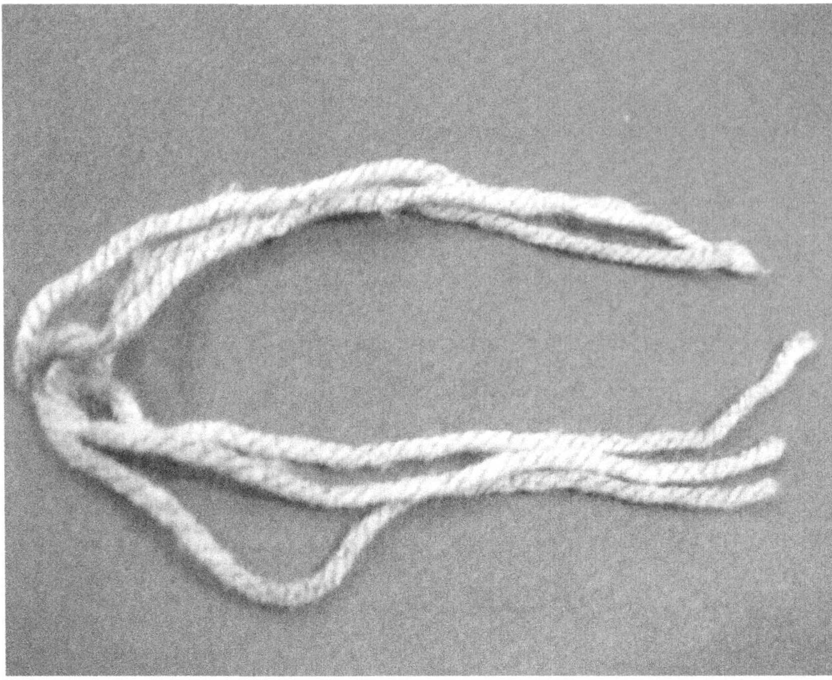

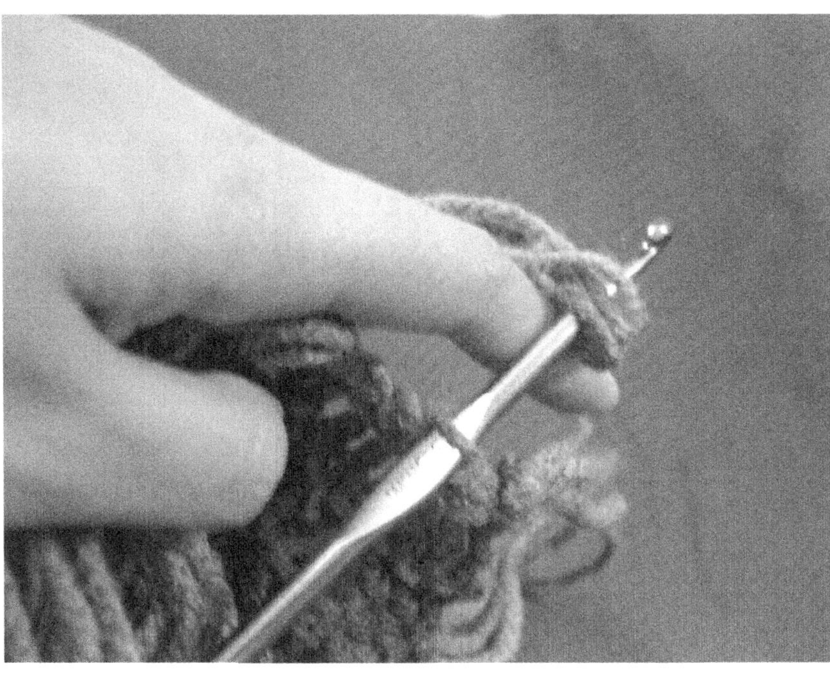

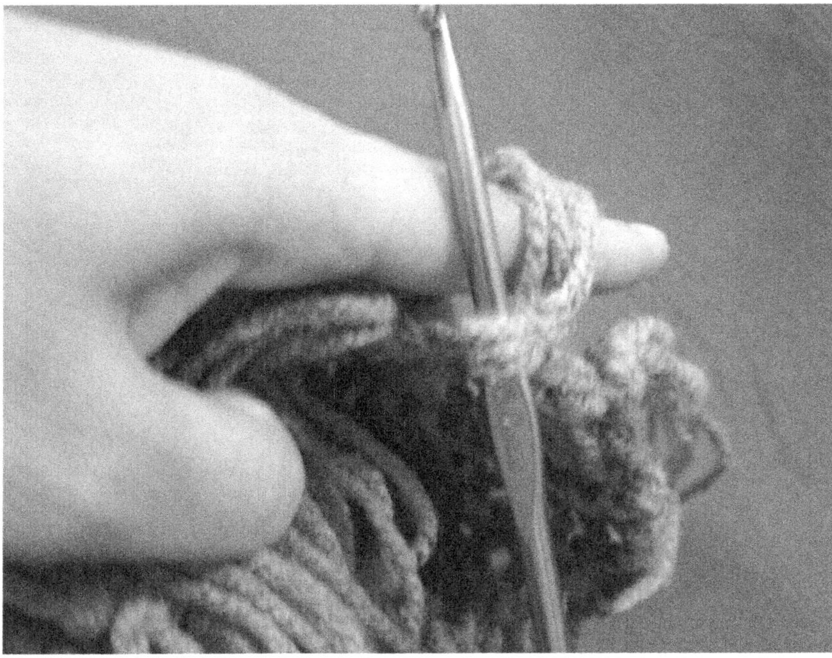

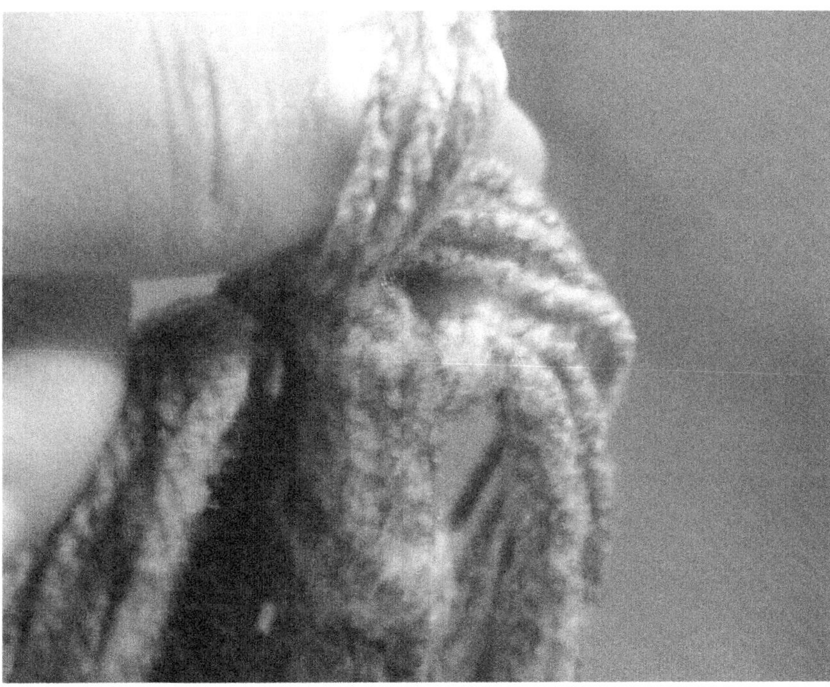

240

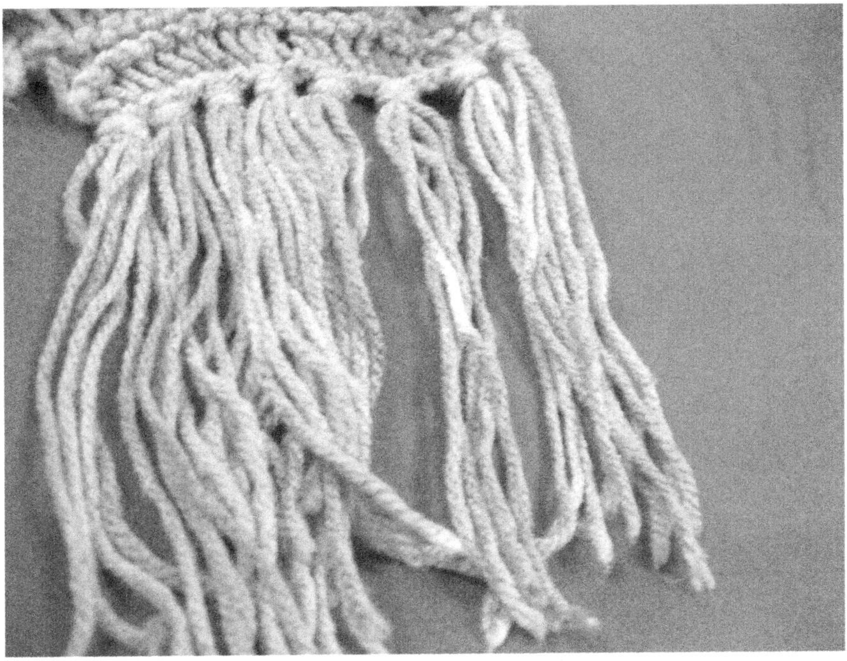

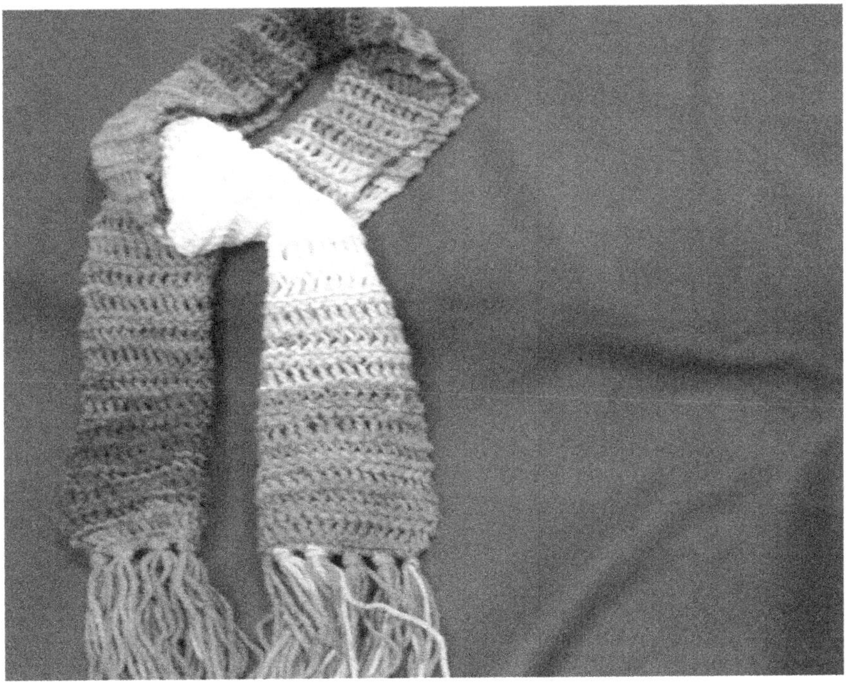

Garter Stitch Baby Blanket

This baby blanket is super easy to make. This makes an amazing gift for anyone, not just new babies in your life.

Materials:

- ❖ Alize 100% acrylic.100 g, 230 yds , pink color

- ❖ Alize 100% acrylic.100 g, 230 yds , white color

- ❖ Alize 100% acrylic.100 g, 230 yds, red color

- ❖ straight knitting needle size 5 mm

- ❖ sewing needle

You can use any combination of colors you want. You can use more than three colors.

Basic Blanket Pattern

This blanket consists of about 56 squares of garter stitched squares.

Each square is 11x11 cm.

There are 19 squares of color A and C, 18 squares of color B.

Cast 18 stitches and knit 34 rows.

Bind off the stitches.

Leave a 20 cm (about 8 inches) tail for use in sewing the square to another square.

244

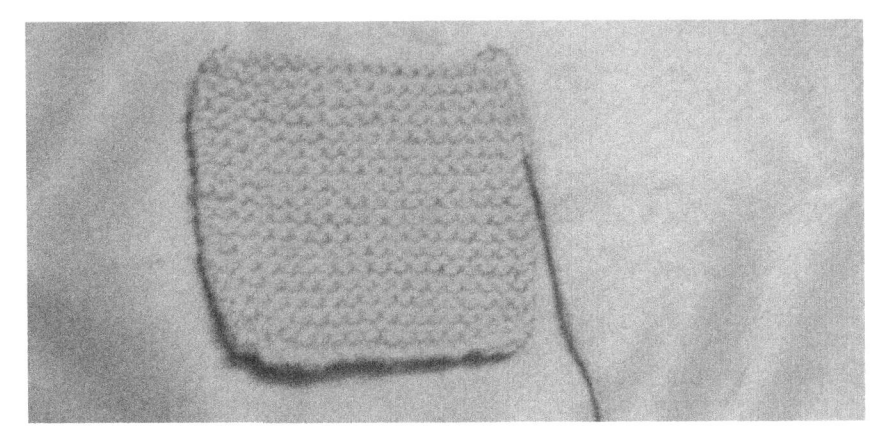

Sew the squares together. The pattern alternates horizontal and vertical orientations. Put one that is vertical beside one that is horizontal and so on.

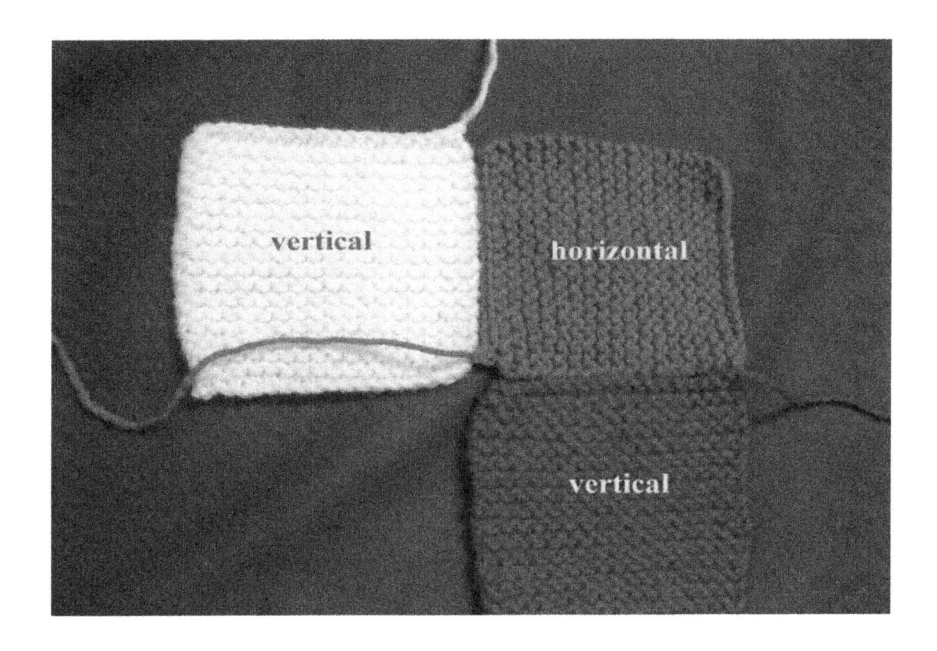

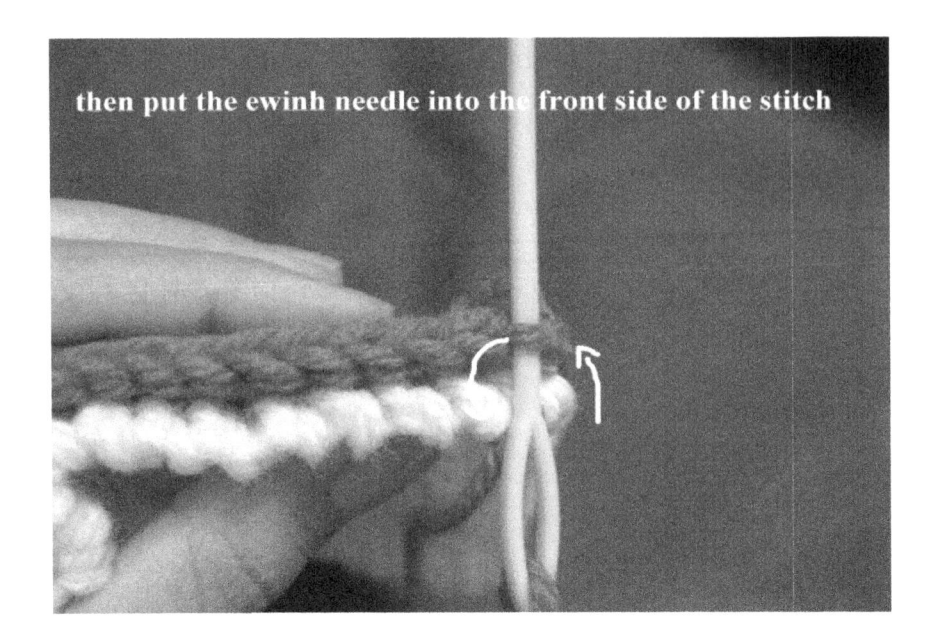

then put the ewinh needle into the front side of the stitch

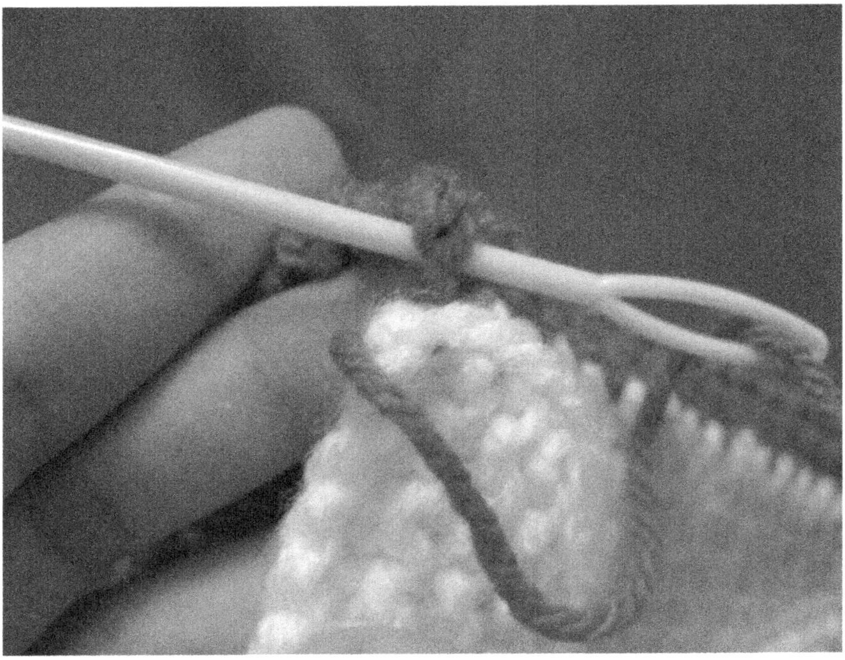

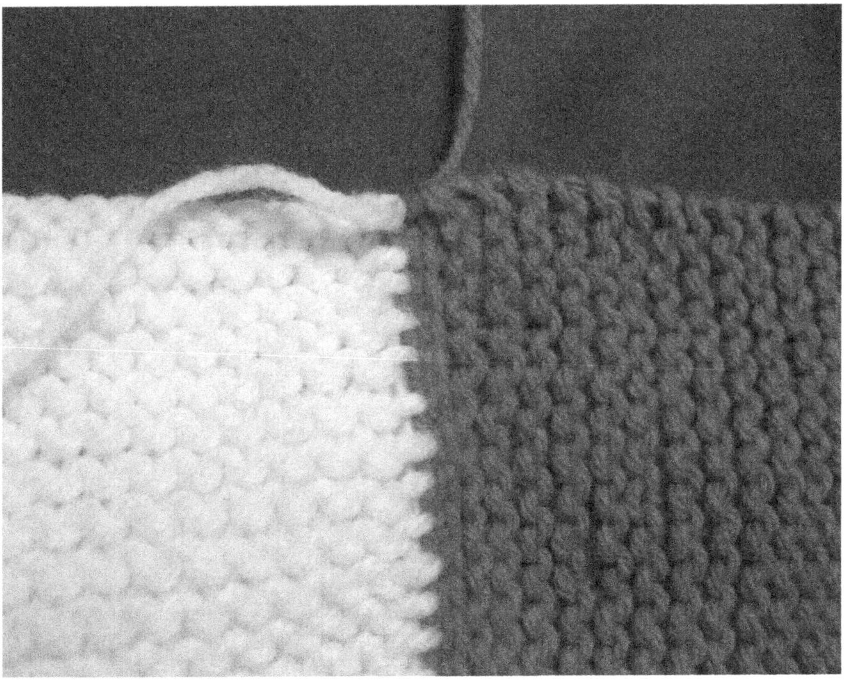

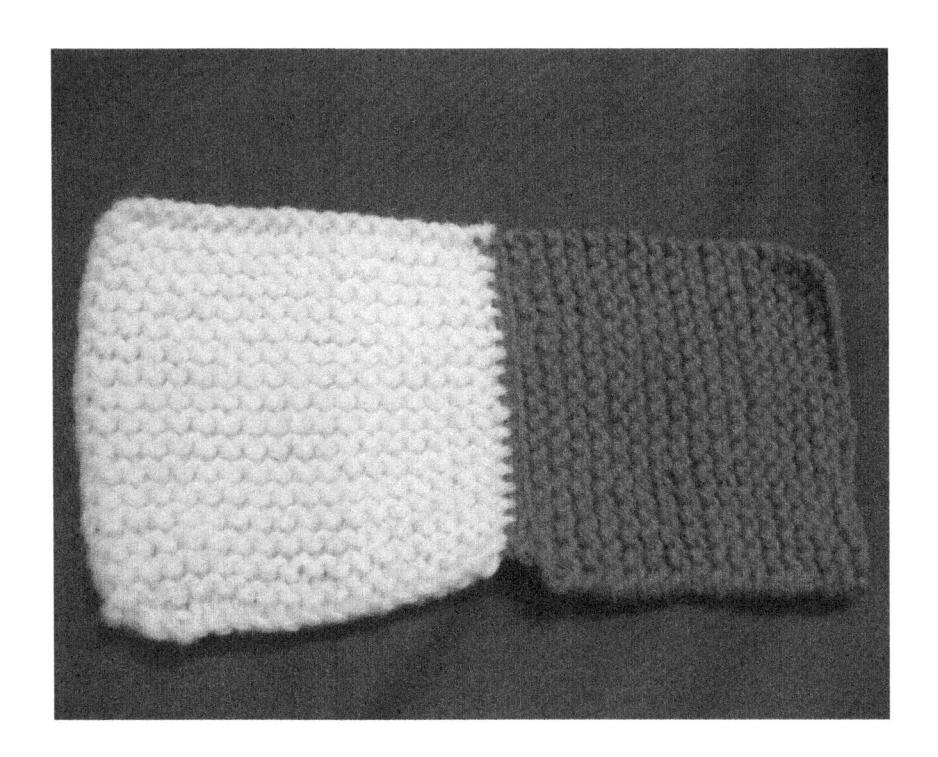

hide the tails in the back by using a crochet hook and cut the rest

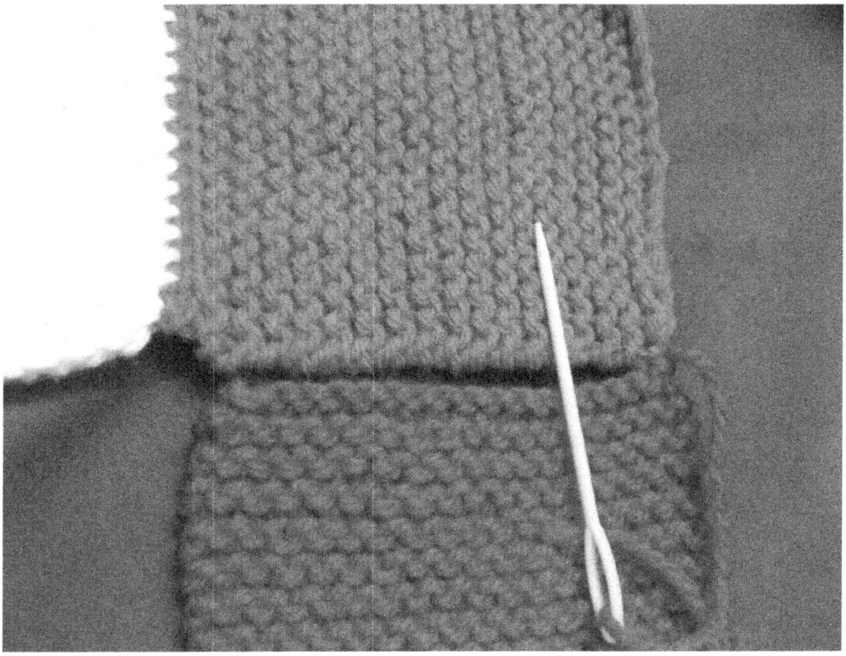

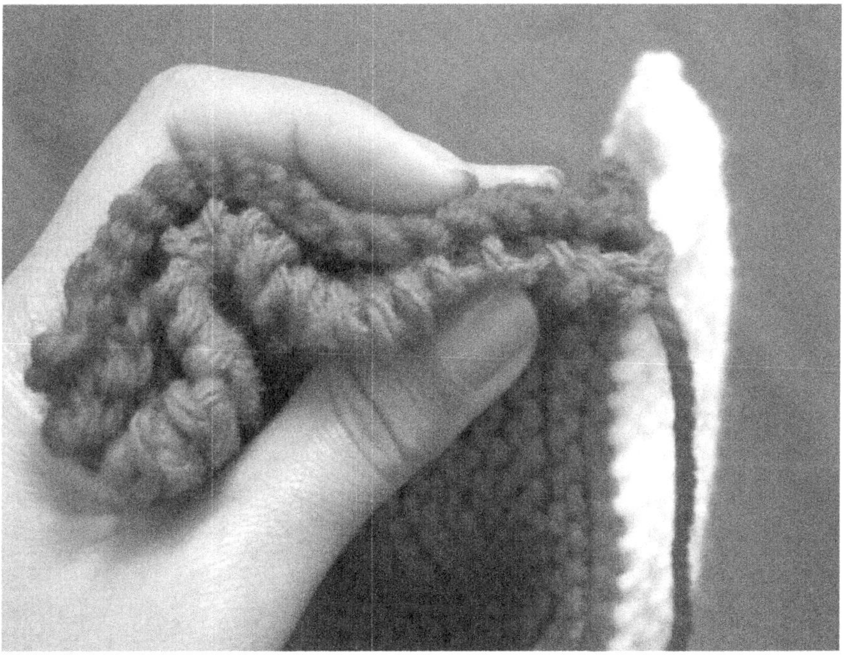

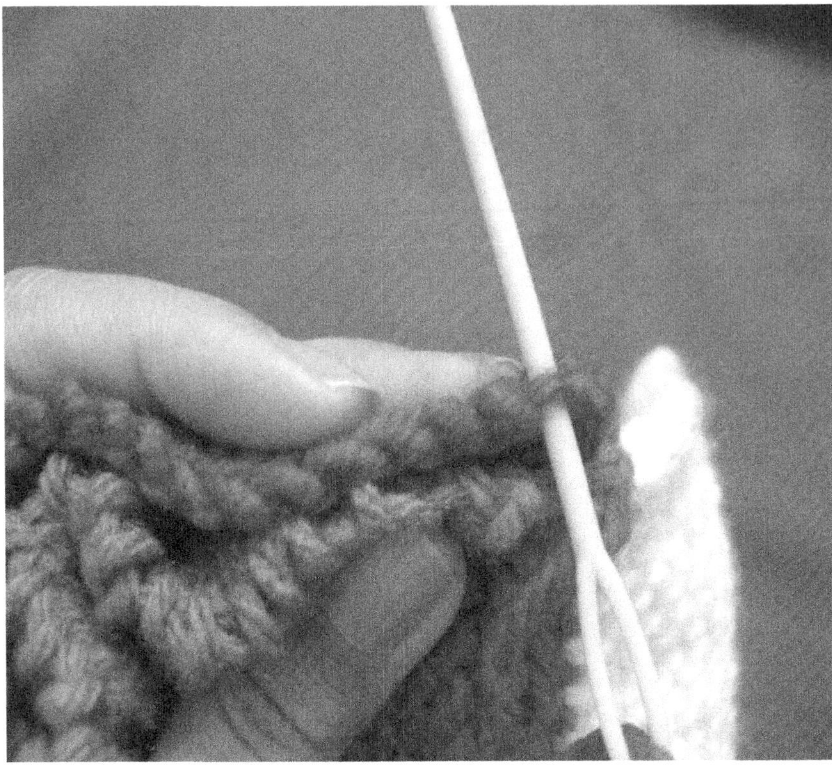

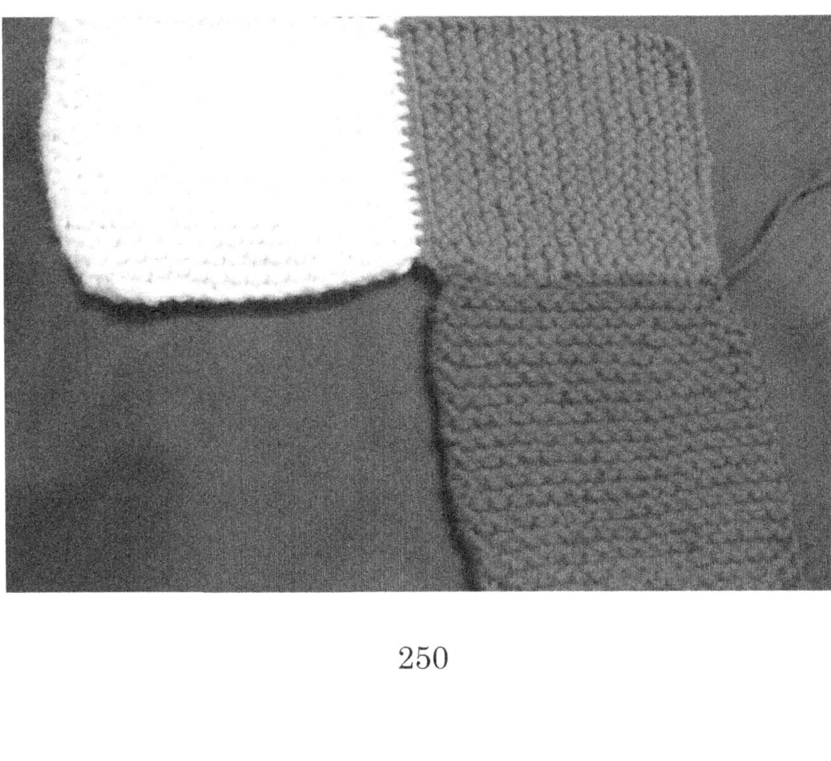

Here is a pattern of the squares:

Use as many squares as you need to make the desired size of the blanket.

Conclusion

I hope you have enjoyed this knitting tutorial book. Creating this guide has certainly been a labor of love for me. I have poured my time, heart, and very soul into this work. Thank you so much for partaking in my love of knitting.

Throughout this book, we have discussed the nitty gritty aspects of knitting anything from lace to baby blankets.

My sincere wish is for you to have taken something meaningful away from reading this knitting guide. My goal is to spread the love of the art of knitting to everyone in the world. I am doing my very best to accomplish this.

Make things! Spread joy! Give gifts!

Handmade knitted goods are the best keepsakes because they were crafted from scratch by your own two hands. You won't find these items in any big box store.

If this book as touched your heart, would you please consider leaving me a review wherever you purchased this book? I will certainly read your feedback and take your comments into consideration. I am hoping to turn this little crafty hobby into something even bigger!

Don't forget, if you need a refresher of the basics of knitting, I have a beginner's tutorial guide in this "Knitting by Pictures" series. Book 1 has all of the starting stitches and how-to laid out in just an easy a format. Maybe it would make a great gift for that up-and-coming knitter in your life.

Happy Knitting!

Made in the USA
Coppell, TX
23 March 2020